FORGE & CARVE

&

CARVE

HERITAGE CRAFTS

THE SEARCH FOR WELL-BEING AND
SUSTAINABILITY IN THE MODERN WORLD

First published in the United Kingdom, 2018, by Canopy Press.
An imprint of 3dtotal Publishing.

Address: 3dtotal.com Ltd, 29 Foregate Street, Worcester, WR1 1DS, United Kingdom.

Correspondence: publishing@3dtotal.com

Website: www.canopy-press.com

ISBN: 978-1-9094-1465-5

Printing and binding: Gomer Press, UK
www.gomer.co.uk

Visit www.canopy-press.com for a complete list of available book titles.

Managing Director: Tom Greenway
Studio Manager: Simon Morse
Assistant Manager: Melanie Robinson
Lead Designer: Imogen Williams
Publishing Manager: Jenny Fox-Proverbs
Template and cover design: Matthew Lewis
Layout: Joseph Cartwright
Illustrations: Marisa Lewis

Back cover photographs (from top to bottom): © Louie Sal-long;
© 3dtotal.com Ltd; © Éamonn O'Sullivan; © Sarah Pike

"I do what I do because of the generosity of others who shared their knowledge freely and I am more than happy to do the same"

Éamonn O'Sullivan

An imprint of 3dtotal Publishing, Canopy Press was established in 2018 to create books focused on traditional crafts, lifestyle, and the environment. With an interest in enjoying the simple things in life, Canopy Press aims to build awareness around sustainable living, a mindful approach to arts and crafts, and an appreciation of the earth we dwell on.

Marrying great aesthetics with enlightening stories from real people, our first title, *Forge & Carve*, presents an insight into heritage crafts and their revival and survival in the modern world. Visit our website and follow us on Instagram to stay up to date with forthcoming books and news.

canopy-press.com | instagram.com/canopypress

CONTENTS

FOREWORD

Robin Wood, MBE

Woodworking, and traditional crafting in general, is going through a renaissance, with a new generation of craftspeople discovering the joys of working wood directly from the trees with simple hand tools. The pioneers of this new culture are renovating old tools and forging new ones. There is a beauty to working this way. The craftspeople of this generation are not backward looking; while many of the techniques they use may be centuries old they also embrace modern technology by using websites, email, and social media to tell the stories behind their work. It is these stories that are so fascinating in a modern context. Increasingly customers are more interested in the stories behind objects than just having the biggest, newest, shiniest things in their home.

It is the stories that make this book particularly special. We hear what makes each craftsperson tick, why they get up in the morning, what motivates them to do what they do. We hear how they got started, what first inspired them, and what they care passionately about. This style of handcrafting is still the road less travelled compared to, for example, the mechanized woodworking that is seen at woodworking shows, but interest is growing exponentially. The artisans of this book are leading the way, showing what is possible, teaching and sharing their knowledge.

One of the most stunning things about heritage crafts is the symbiotic and evolutionary relationship between different disciplines. For example, woodworkers could not exist without tool makers. Learning how to correctly sharpen a tool so that it leaves a silky clean-cut surface is an incredibly empowering experience. One step further is learning to make your own tools. Many tool makers today started out as woodworkers, made tools for themselves, then for friends, and finally produced tools for others too. It is one of the beauties of this field that there is a great interplay and ongoing conversation between tool makers and tool users. This feedback loop makes for better tools but also adds meaning to using a tool when you know the person that made it.

The story we have been told about making things is that larger scale is always more efficient. The craftspeople here however show that small is possible and small is splendid. With low overheads, a few simple tools, and plenty of skill and passion, the makers can create objects of profound beauty and meaning. They are connected to their raw materials and understand the impact of their work on the planet, cutting wood from sustainably managed woodlands or using ethically sourced leather to make objects that will last a lifetime.

People have become used to the cheap "throwaway" culture that exists today, knowing that most things they buy will be in a landfill in a few years' time. At the same time, stories of the working conditions in which things are made overseas prick the collective conscience. The craftspeople in this book offer an alternative: the opportunity to buy from a known passionate maker, to experience the whole story of how and why the thing was made. Like the early pioneers of the organic food movement they are not in it for profit; it is more of a lifestyle or moral choice, something they wholeheartedly believe in. And increasingly others are joining them.

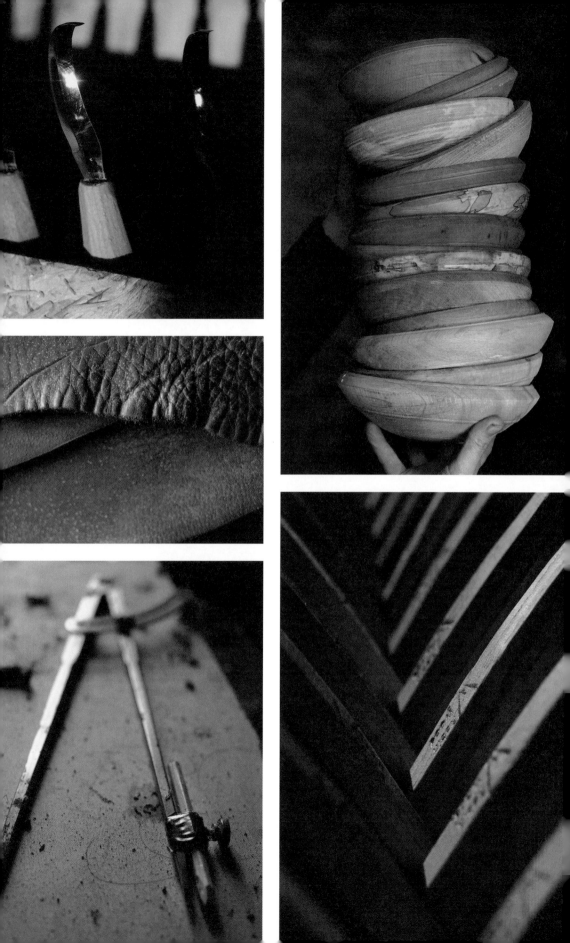

MY JOURNEY INTO THE WOODS

Tom Greenway | Founder, Canopy Press

My expedition into traditional crafting began on a mundane car journey down the M5 in Worcestershire when I spotted a sign saying "woodland for sale". That got me thinking. How wonderful would it be to have your own patch of woodland, an escape where you could immerse yourself in nature and rekindle your childhood? Memories of making hazel-stick bows and arrows, dens, and campfires with the likes of Ben Orford (meet Ben on page 42) and his older brothers sprung to mind. "That's it," I decided, "I'm going to buy myself a wood!"

It took one year to find a suitable plot that was local to me. It was four acres in the middle of a much bigger wood, and full of large sweet chestnut trees. "They're really nice," I thought, not knowing the first thing about sweet chestnut being favoured for certain crafts and coppice workers. The entire four acres were also thick with invasive cherry laurel, now some thirty feet tall. "I should be able to clear that in a few days," I naively speculated (anyone familiar with woodland management will know that this is not the case).

In spite of my initial ignorance, I had started my journey, a journey that would dabble in bushcraft, conservation, foraging, outdoor cooking, and, most importantly to me, craft. I had a longing to just "make stuff" and I also needed a plan to rope in labour to help clear those strangled woods. My wonderful parents were the first onboard and helped tirelessly, but we still needed more hands. I posted a potential group on the popular Meetup website (meetup.com) to get things started. I ambitiously called it "Worcester Traditional Crafts" but it has since become more affectionately known as "Wood Club".

To entice willing volunteers to follow vague directions to find a slightly feral man in the middle of a wood, I needed a bit of an incentive. I started participating in other crafters' courses, researching and buying a few tools, with the hope of showing people in turn how to carve spoons, make wooden stools, taper a stick into a bow, and anything else that seemed appealing enough for them to come and trade their time to help with the woodland management. It worked well: in the mornings the laurel was hacked and slashed with great enthusiasm. People were starting to share my "escape" – who knows what those IT workers and school teachers were imagining as they ferociously attacked gnarly laurel trunks with hooks and axes. In the afternoons, many beautiful items were crafted, and also numerous items labelled with other names – "rustic", "unique", "interesting", and "special to you" were some of the terms bandied about. But it didn't really matter; everyone just seemed so happy.

"The realization that you have suddenly removed plastic, waste, money, transportation, and consumerism from the equation in one pleasant afternoon in the woods is without doubt a joyful thing"

One of my favourite things to see was a newcomer to the group who, not quite being sure what to make, would go for the "make a thick stick thinner" project, and sometimes even clutch their thin stick masterpiece when leaving the woods to take home and enthusiastically show their loved ones. How could even the simplest of craft projects create such satisfaction? I think there is an inherent connection with using our hands to create useful objects that still lies within all of us. This is how we used to survive; it was literally life or death. Reducing the size of a stick using the therapeutic method of effortlessly removing slender shavings one after the other with a drawknife and shavehorse creates the foundation for many things: a spatula to cook with, a leg for a stool, a bow to hunt with, or a bobbin to weave with, to name but a few. The realization that you have suddenly removed plastic, waste, money, transportation, and consumerism from the equation in one pleasant afternoon in the woods is without doubt a joyful thing.

At the hobbyist level, crafting is experiencing a renaissance driven in part by modern media sharing and teaching techniques – YouTube and Instagram are perfect examples, with hundreds of crafters sharing high-quality photos of their wares and passing on their knowledge. At the same time, too much modern media is also fuelling the need to craft as a form of escapism from a hectic, modern-day life. Finding inner well-being from craft is a key benefit of the movement, in a time in which mindfulness and an appreciation of the simple things are held in high regard. It is certainly the case in my experience that crafts offer a much-needed outlet for creativity and open up doors for new ways of living. Another issue the craft renaissance brings to the fore is the value of knowledge. In 2003, UNESCO introduced the Convention for the Safeguarding of Intangible Cultural Heritage, focusing not just on the conservation of items produced by heritage crafts but on the importance of passing on the knowledge and expertise behind them. Over a hundred countries agreed to this convention, although as currently stands the UK is not one of these. We hope that through this book we are aiding the movement to preserve those century-old skills.

Forge & Carve aims to show an overview of a range of disciplines so that readers can see which ones pique their interest to perhaps pursue further. Crafters talk about their starting points, motivations, challenges, and successes, and also provide a brief outline of their process so you can gain an idea of what is involved. The progression from hobbyist, to selling a few items, to professional craftsperson, is a dream for many, and this book is a showcase of eighteen heritage crafters who have achieved such a level. The title *Forge & Carve*, besides the obvious literal connotations, represents the forging and carving of a career; through these pages we hope to demonstrate how people are making traditional crafted items and also making a living from them in the twenty-first century.

You have to be savvy – marketing and promotional methods have changed a lot, and the need for the items has also changed in a way that means they can now can be art pieces as well as functional items; some customers may want a learning experience rather than an already finished item; you therefore need to be familiar with your modern-day audience. The willingness of the artisans featured here to share their tips and tricks for success is a credit to the entire crafting movement. To them, the more people who participate, trade, share, and learn, the bigger the cake and the more slices for everyone to enjoy.

The journey of this book starts from right here on our doorstep in Herefordshire, UK. We had a wonderful time visiting knife-making and leather-working team Ben and Lois Orford (pages 42 and 154) and coracle maker Peter Faulkner (page 184). Their enthusiasm was infectious, and we hope we have captured that successfully through the following pages. We then spoke to craftspeople from further afield, including a woodturner from Bavaria and a trug maker in New Zealand. The types of crafts and location shared here vary wildly but, as you will discover, the common elements of passion, community, well-being, and education repeatedly shine through. Our goal is for you, the reader, to follow this journey, be inspired, and maybe start your own adventure. Together we can fuel the revival of the crafting movement even further.

"It is my belief that the making of things by hand is one of the core elements of being human – the act of engaging in craft brings all of your senses into play"

EJ Osborne

BLACKSMITHING

Blacksmiths work with iron or steel by heating it up to a malleable level using a forge and then striking or bending the metal into shape. Although the craft has been developed over thousands of years, the basic techniques remain the same, with the unmistakable sound of hammer on metal. From their forge, blacksmiths can produce small items, such as coat hooks, horse shoes, and gardening tools, all the way up to fences, gates, and railings.

"I am constantly surprised by the sophistication and complexity of metal items produced with the most basic of blacksmithing tools"

Matt Jenkins

MATT JENKINS

Manitoba, Canada | cloverdaleforge.com

Training: Self-taught + Degree in Mechanical Engineering

Matt Jenkins set up Cloverdale Forge with fellow blacksmith and wife, Karen Rudolph, and makes forged metal items including hooks, brackets, belt buckles, tools, and bottle openers. Winner of the first-place medal in Drawing and Design in the 2015 World Forging Championship in Stia, Italy, Matt uses early industrial tools and techniques to produce functional items that appeal to contemporary consumers.

ORIGINS

The month I was born, my father made the decision to jump careers and interview for a position with Parks Canada as a historic blacksmith. When asked if he had experience in blacksmithing, he simply replied: "We have a forge on the farm." He conveniently forgot to mention he had never used the forge or an anvil, except to squash the occasional wood tick, and since the interviewer didn't ask any follow-up questions, he was awarded the position.

Eighteen years later, when I was in need of a summer job, I applied for the same blacksmith position at Lower Fort Garry National Historic Site in Saint Andrews, Manitoba. During the interview I was asked if I knew how to blacksmith; I answered the same way my father did: "We have a forge on the farm." At the time I had not yet picked up a hammer to forge anything, but over the course of seven summers – through trial and many errors – I gained a basic understanding of how to work iron into functional items.

I was bitten by the iron bug, and blacksmithing became part of my life. I spent much of my twenties and thirties connecting with blacksmiths around the world, continuing to build upon the skills and techniques I acquired while working as a historic blacksmith. Eventually, the creative and artistic aspects of blacksmithing lured me away from my career as a mechanical engineer. In 2016 my business partner and wife, Karen, launched Cloverdale Forge into a full-time business.

MOTIVATIONS

Blacksmithing is one of the most self-reliant trades, with most of the tools required for the craft made by the blacksmith for the blacksmith. This self-reliance is the base of my interest and what I enjoy most about the work. It is inspiring to think about the history of the trade – the further back in time, the fewer tools and technologies there were available, and the more creative smiths had to be able to engineer the material for final products. The simplest of tools or jigs I build in my shop today reflect that history.

"It is more than just hammering. It is the ability to manifest an idea into life"

Making a living using your hands as an artisan is many times more centred on a lifestyle than an income bracket. That lifestyle includes a strong sense of community among makers. For me that extends beyond those living in the Winnipeg and Manitoba region to include folks from around the globe; staying in contact is easy through modern communications.

Blacksmithing is physically tough on one's body, but for me, it is more than just hammering. It is the ability to manifest an idea into life. Taking a thought, sketching it onto paper, then manipulating steel to become the physical item, is one of the reasons I enjoy walking out to my shop and starting my daily forge. Making a living as a blacksmith provides a balance between my engineering brain and my creative brain.

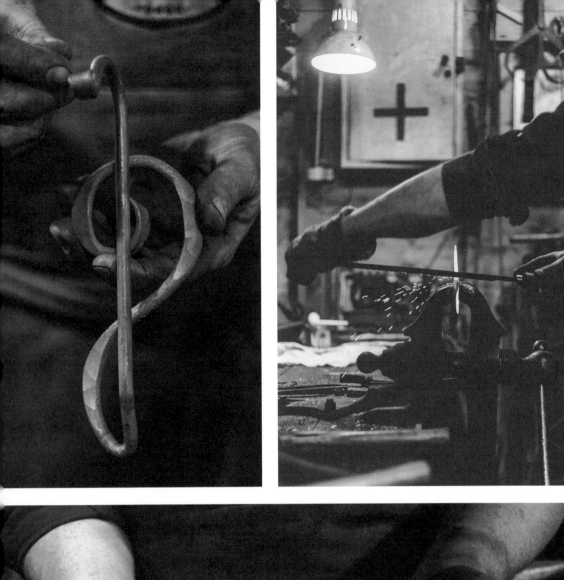

WORKSPACE AND TOOLS

My shop is located on my family's farm, and is approximately 400 square feet in size, with a dirt floor and no heat. It is bitterly cold in the winter and full of mosquitoes in the summer, but the small space serves me well. Initially built by my grandfather as a maintenance shed for farming equipment, my father repurposed it when I was fourteen by setting up a bare-bones blacksmith forge. Since moving back to Manitoba from the Southern US in 2006, I have slowly made the place my own; not only with the tools inside but over time I have replaced three walls and the roof. It is cosy, allowing for tools to be close at hand when needed.

Anvil, forge, hammer, and steel are all it takes to bring the craft of blacksmithing to life. However, a blacksmith can never have too many tools. I believe the best jobs require the making of new tools or jigs. But new tools in a small space come with the extra challenge of figuring out where to store them when not in use!

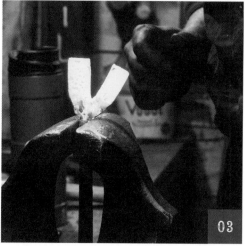

PROCESS OVERVIEW

01 Here you can see the process for creating three fire tools: a poker, shovel, and tongs. Custom projects start in the shop with a soapstone sketch on a metal layout table. Mild steel is then cut to a rough length using a metal bandsaw.

02 With the raw metal cut to length, we are ready to start forging, the process of forming and shaping hot metal. The first step is to draw out the long tapered handles on the three fire tools. I leave an isolated mass of steel at the end of each, which will provide material for the functional parts of the fire tools.

03 For the poker, the isolated steel mass needs to split into a fork shape. The splitting is

accomplished with a "hot chisel." Hot chisels are used by blacksmiths to cut and shape red-hot steel, which is much softer than cold steel. A hot chisel is not typically hardened or tempered and features a ground blade, which means it rides flush against the surface of the anvil. Once divided, the two prongs provide material for both the spike and a barb. The ends are then drawn out to delicate points and shaped for functionality.

04 The shovel requires extra material to be "fire" or "forge welded" onto the end of the handle to accommodate the creation of the shovel pan. Forge welding has been used since ancient times. During the process, a blacksmith secures two pieces of metal together by heating them to a

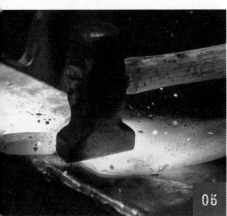

high temperature and hammering so the two become one.

05 To create the shovel, the material must be hammered into a flat and consistent thickness. Top tools come in various shapes and sizes depending on the job. Top tools are held against the metal being forged, as seen in image 05, and are used when an exact hammer blow is required. In image 05, the top tool is used to creatively define the transition between the handle and the shovel pan.

06 Once the shovel pan is drawn out and flattened to its approximate size, measurements are taken and laid out with chalk. The final shovel is then trimmed with a "cold chisel". Cold chisels are

used for cutting cold metal; they are usually shorter in length compared to hot chisels. Made from high carbon tool steel, the blade is typically hardened to keep a sharp edge. After the shovel pan is cut to shape, the sides are cleaned up with a hand file so that no sharp edges remain.

07 The final step in forging the shovel pan is to heat up the trimmed metal and form the shovel shape using a series of anvil stakes. Just like hammers, anvils come with different shapes and surfaces. Each anvil stake is designed to perform specific tasks that allow blacksmiths to shape the metal into curved or straight shapes. Anvil stakes are smaller than a traditional anvil and usually fit into a vice or the hardy hole of a larger anvil.

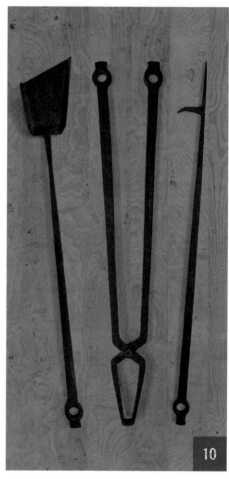

08 The tongs are forged from two pieces of steel and riveted together. The raw metal starts the same length and size; both pieces are drawn out to form a long taper and bent into shape by hammering the hot metal over the anvil horn.

09 Holes are needed to create room for the hinge pin on the tongs. These holes are made using a slot punch, instead of a drill press. This process allows blacksmiths to punch a half-inch hole in a half-inch square bar as it doesn't remove any material and instead displaces it outward. A drill press removes stock from the metal bar. This is the same process that produced the holes in the ends of the handles of the fire tools.

10 Once each element is complete, I finish the toolset by painting each piece with a clear enamel finish to protect against rusting and oxidation.

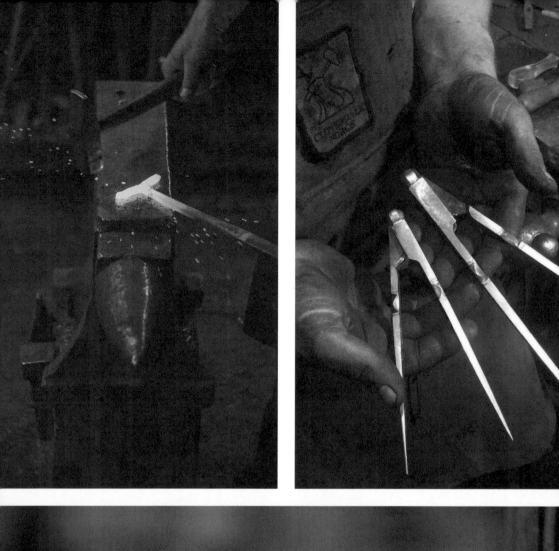

FORGING A CAREER

Although I have been blacksmithing for over twenty-five years, Cloverdale Forge did not become my full-time focus until the spring of 2016. Leaping from hobbyist to full-time artisan should be considered carefully. A maker business requires a full array of skills beyond that of producing objects. One has to schedule the time to attain buyers – whether it is custom work or wholesale orders – and once you have them, time must be allocated to communicate on the status of their projects. To keep business flowing, Cloverdale Forge relies on emails, texts, and online software for email blasts, invoicing, and project management. Together these tools afford more time in the shop versus the office management and paperwork side of the business.

Although no expert, as I am still learning the business side of blacksmithing, I would encourage those looking to make a living with their hands to search out as many business advisors as possible. Find mentors who are available when tough business decisions are required. If mentors are hard to find where you live, use online tools that have been developed to help small business owners. Running a business as an independent craftsperson means a surprising amount of time is spent outside your studio, communicating with the clients you already have and hustling to land the projects you want in the future. As another piece of advice, get into the habit early of tracking the time it takes to complete tasks – knowing this will allow you to price projects wisely. It is easy to get so involved with a project that you forget to track the hours. The workload leaves little downtime – to quote my wife, "the beautiful thing about being a small business owner is the flexibility of getting to choose which eighteen hours a day you work".

I start most mornings eating breakfast with my business partner (and wife), during which we outline the day's required tasks and action plan. From there, I work on sketches and communications – then it is out to the forge to hammer. I usually end the work day by posting a picture of what I am working on to a variety of social media platforms. This daily visual journal has been an excellent way to educate those interested in the craft on the processes and techniques that go into making a piece. It is also exciting for clients to see their project coming together.

Most businesses face annual business cycles that leave the owners with too much or too little work. My father always said, "if you get us some steel wool, we can knit you a Volkswagen," although no one has yet to take us up on the offer. We have been able to maintain a steady workflow by mixing our income streams between wholesale orders, custom work, teaching at blacksmith workshops, and selling at markets. Currently I am focused on developing the North American market by searching for retail spaces that focus on the aesthetics of handmade goods.

SURVIVING IN THE MODERN WORLD

Telling the story of how a maker shapes objects into existence is a large part of surviving as a business today. Beyond the look and feel of a product, there is a particular aesthetic intertwined when a shopper buys from a maker. That history (or story) of the article is of significant value.

Years before Cloverdale Forge had an official website, I set up Instagram, Facebook, Twitter, and Tumblr accounts. These sites create and sustain a dialogue about my work. Conversations on design and inquiries about techniques helped in the process of producing an item. The daily visual story told through social media provides a friendly way to educate potential clients on the hours required as well as give aspiring metal artists insight into the tools used when creating custom ironwork. Through social media, craft has become relatable, and many of the mysteries of making have disappeared.

In 2016, I took on a year-long creative project in which I designed, forged, and posted a different style of hook every day of the year. I relied on social media to document my work; each hook was labelled with the "#366hooks" hashtag (366 instead of 365 because 2016 was a leap year). Marking all of the hooks under one unified hashtag continues to provide a simple way to find each hook created during that year. Some days I would barely finish my hook by midnight. As the year progressed, the hook project grew a loyal base of followers from around the world, and many are still engaged with my work.

CONSERVING THE CRAFT AND ITS LIVELIHOOD

When I first got into blacksmithing, information on the craft was hard to find. When travelling, I would always take time to stop at used-book stores and antique shops, in the hope of finding a discontinued book on metalwork or a discarded tool. Now it seems that everyone has tiny computers in their pockets which allow those interested in blacksmithing to watch YouTube videos that explain various techniques. Tool and book retailers are also online. The interconnectedness that we live with today has increased awareness through access and education. Because the traditional skills and methods of blacksmiths were almost lost to history, with a resurgence in the seventies, there is now an openness to pass along the "how-to" knowledge within the blacksmithing community. This openness extends to the exploration of new techniques and approaches to the material, which I believe is unique to the craft of blacksmithing.

"To keep the craft alive, you must let the craft live outside the bounds of history"

Blacksmithing is the most primitive form of ironworking. This description poisons people's opinion of a blacksmith's work. I am constantly surprised by the sophistication and complexity of metal items produced with the most basic of blacksmithing tools. If the skills of blacksmithing are not passed on, then all that remains are the primitive tools and the public's expectation of raw and unpolished work from the modern blacksmith.

A host of other metalworking trades have evolved from what was once the domain of the blacksmith. When a new tool or innovation came to light, it was split off into a speciality – this is one of the reasons that there are now locksmiths, gunsmiths, welders, and machinists. All of these have slowly stripped away a lot of the industrial uses for the blacksmith. In modern times, most of what remains is the art of the blacksmith.

As critical as the traditional skills and techniques are to learning the craft of blacksmithing, there should also be room to embrace modern and appropriate technologies which continue to advance the craft. Without innovation in blacksmithing, the most primitive form of metalwork becomes static, and those sophisticated pieces made by the craftsman become only museum relics. To keep the craft alive, you must let the craft live outside the bounds of history.

KNIFE MAKING

Knives are the most basic yet essential tool for many heritage crafts, used for whittling, carving, cutting, and removing bark from green wood for a variety of items. They are also a symbol of survival; for thousands of years knives in some form have been used in the making of shelter and the gathering and preparation of food. In terms of craftsmanship, knives exquisitely combine contrasting materials – such as wood and metal – requiring very different skill sets to master.

"A knife is the most fundamental tool to a human – from the very first blade made from a shard of flint to the latest modern steel; without a cutting tool no craft is possible"

Ben Orford

BEN ORFORD

Herefordshire, UK | benandloisorford.com

Training: City & Guilds in Cabinet & Furniture Design + Apprenticeship in Green
Woodworking, Woodland Crafts & Woodland Management

**Ben works with his wife Lois in a stylish converted barn in the Herefordshire hills (meet Lois
Orford on page 154). Together they create bushcraft tools including knives and axes, with
Ben crafting the tools and Lois creating the leather sheaths to place them in. With training
in green woodwork, woodland management, and blacksmithing, Ben's experience is eclectic
and extensive, which brings an impressive level of understanding of the materials and tools
he works with, matched only by his skill and passion for his craft.**

ORIGINS

Brought up on a farm, as a child I could regularly be found playing in the woods and going on camping
holidays. This meant I always had knives on my person although I could never afford a good one. My
father worked on vintage cars, which gave me access to a workshop, and at sixteen I made my first
knife – a Bowie knife – out of an old file to take camping with me. It was too big and cumbersome to
be very practical, but was a great start to my knife-making journey.

My interest in hands-on activities continued, and I initially learned green woodworking, making
objects like spoons, chairs, and tables. Tool-making came about through wanting a knife optimized
for certain tasks, such as spoon carving. In this way making knives and green woodworking are
symbiotic for me. I'm able to make better knives because I know what they will be used for. Tool-
making also allowed me to use beautiful off-cuts from chairs that were just the right size for a knife
handle, ensuring minimum amounts of material go to waste.

MOTIVATIONS

One of the main things I love about knife making is that it involves working with a range of materials that put to use a whole host of skills. You're working with wood, steel, leather – sometimes even antler. The mix of organic elements blended together in harmony is stunning. There is also still the child alchemist inside me that adores plunging cherry-red metal into oil and seeing golden sparks fly off the metal as you grind it. I am fascinated with the science behind the processes of heating and cooling metal.

The connection back to our ancestors is another fantastic element that is common among all heritage crafts. A knife is the most fundamental tool to a human – from the very first blade made from a shard of flint to the latest modern steel; without a cutting tool no craft is possible. The idea of gathering resources, being outdoors, and making something useful to help us survive is a primeval urge that is incredible to return to. I was fortunate in that I had a holistic apprenticeship that combined green woodworking with coppicing, which allowed me to experience both the collecting and crafting of wood. Lois and I used money from our wedding to plant trees on our land, and these are now old enough to harvest wood that is perfect for carving spoons from.

"What we create is in us, and is something that I would not be myself without"

For me, however, the buzz of creativity – taking something organic and putting your influence on it – is what really stands out about heritage crafts. The materials tell you what they want you to do with them rather than the opposite; every piece of wood is different and I have to decide how best to carve it to make the knife handle I want. What we create is in us, and is something that I would not be myself without. I find myself becoming jittery if I haven't made something in a while; I constantly need that adrenaline rush of creativity.

It is this creativity that drives me – and I believe any maker – to carry on. There is a five-minute window when you have finished something when you can enjoy what you have made. After that you start seeing areas you could have done differently and decide that the next knife you will make will be perfect. Of course it isn't in my eyes, but it is this ongoing search for improvement that drives us. Practice and repetition is how you master a craft and a material.

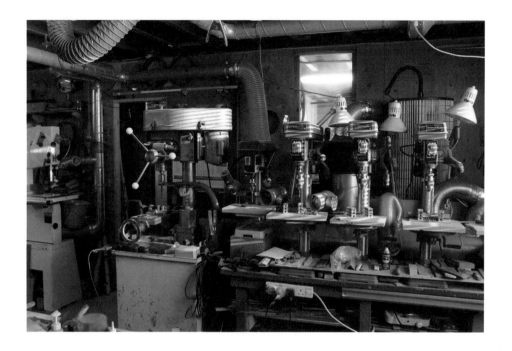

WORKSPACE AND TOOLS

The environment we work in definitely has an impact on our productivity. An incredible view of the Herefordshire countryside and interesting decor means we are never short of inspiration. I don't think we could create what we create if we were on an industrial estate.

I use a lot of modern machinery such as electric drills and bandsaws, which some could argue take away from the essence of heritage crafts. However it still comes down to working with raw materials and making every piece individually. We have to adapt and if there is a tool that will allow me to do something better and quicker, I will use it. Saving time on these areas allows me to spend more time on the areas where original craftsmanship really shines.

I have numerous drills which allow me to drill different-sized holes quickly without having to change the drill bit each time. I also have an anvil, a mark of the blacksmithing parts of my job. The middle-left image on the next page shows the tool I use to add our logo to each knife – seven tonnes of pressure are exerted to make this possible. The top-right image shows a Rockwell hardness tester, which I use to check the hardness of the metal at various stages. Choosing the wood for a knife is one of the hardest things I have to do as there are so many beautiful options offering different potential; I keep a range of offcuts – including ash, elm, maple, birch, English walnut, and Arizona desert ironwood – in a heated cupboard where they can dry out properly.

PROCESS OVERVIEW

01 I use a stock removal process for creating the basic knife shape from the steel. This involves taking a ruler width of steel, scribing the design using a carbide scribe, and then roughly removing all the bits that don't look like a knife using a bandsaw.

02 I use a coarse-grit grinder with a P36 grit belt to remove extra steel down to the outline I scribed. This is when the sparks begin to fly! I drill holes through the steel which I will use to clamp the blade and handle together later. These holes will also affect the weight and balance of the knife.

03 Next I scribe out the bevels using measuring tools and roughly grind them, leaving the edge

thick. The blade isn't functional at this point; the steel is still quite malleable as it is annealed. This means I can do all the work I need to do at this stage, such as drill the holes and stamp our logo.

04 Once I've added our logo to the blade, I take the soft steel and run it through a series of controlled heats to make it very hard, and then stress relieve it to turn it from glass-hard to soft enough to sharpen it to a usable tool. This involves using an electric kiln, plunging the metal into vegetable oil to cool it, and then baking at a much lower temperature for a much longer length of time. I then grind the bevels to refine them so the knife is sharp.

05 The wood needs to be very dry in order to stay flat and be a good fit to the tang. I want the grain to line up with the direction of the blade, so with the wood split into two pieces I position one piece according to the grain and clamp the blade on top. I can then transpose the holes from the blade to the handle material, which will be fixed in place using trial pins.

06 I angle the front edges of the handle by thirty degrees as it will not be possible to do this once it is attached to the blade. I roughly saw off any excess wood using a bandsaw, and then use two-part epoxy, screws, and bolts to attach the two handle slabs onto the knife blade.

07 Once the epoxy has dried, the whole knife can be taken to the grinder to remove excess material, rounding and sculpting the handle to the right shape. I then begin to sand it by hand working my way down various grits.

08 I dip the wood in linseed oil to help bring out the colour and grain, soaking it overnight. After leaving it to dry for a few days, I give it a final buff and apply wax to seal the wood.

09 I peel the tape off the blade that I had used to protect it while working on the handle, and give it one more sharpen. I want the knife to be as high a quality as possible for the customer so I can spend a long time perfecting it at the end.

FORGING A CAREER

I never consciously made the decision to turn tool-making into a full-time job; it evolved naturally. I knew after leaving school I needed to do something practical. I found my way onto a three-year green woodwork apprenticeship and went self-employed once this was completed, mainly making furniture and providing training courses myself. During this time, people would attend a chair-making course for the first time, for example, and wouldn't have a knife, so I gave them mine; they liked it, asked where it came from, and wanted to buy one. I saw a gap in the market and moved from making chairs to making tools. It's easier to work with something small as it can easily be posted anywhere around the world.

"If what you produce is high quality and you make yourself and your brand known, you can get to where you want to be"

Our business also grew organically, with us starting out by going to shows and trying to sell our tools there. UK shows such as The Bushcraft Show and Wilderness Gathering were key in getting our products and name out there. It's important to persevere – if you have a roof over your head and are able to survive, keep following your heart. Don't think about earning a living; think about doing something that stimulates you. You don't need extra money to go to the cinema when you're doing something that you really enjoy. If what you produce is high quality and you make yourself and your brand known, you can get to where you want to be.

I love making the elaborate, expensive products but our mainstay is the small carving tools that people need regularly. It is important to understand what the market wants and work with that. Often we find that someone will buy a small cheaper tool to start with, see and appreciate the brand, and save up for a more expensive one. Our brand is integral to who we are.

Obviously you need to be driven if you are going to be self-employed. Motivation is never a problem for me – it's almost the opposite; I can't normally turn the creative part of my brain off so it can be difficult to have a break. Knife ideas and designs often come to me in the middle of the night and I initially have to jot them down on a napkin or whatever I have to hand. Going for a walk can be a good reset. I find myself still crafting in the evening but working on personal items instead, trying new techniques I would like to explore.

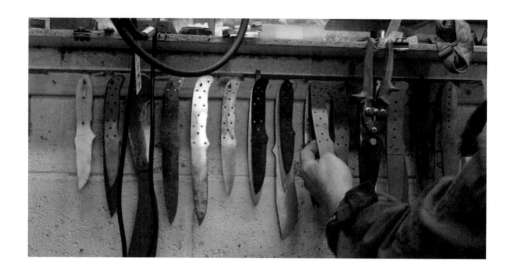

SURVIVING IN THE MODERN WORLD

Technological advancements and increased accessibility offer many benefits to traditional craftspeople. The growth of social media and being able to easily ship worldwide has seen our sales soar. It was a family member who encouraged us to make the most of Instagram and YouTube, and this was definitely the right advice. The increase in demand means we can now bulk order material, which makes it more economical (obviously where we can make something from our own wood we do). Everything used to be cut out by hand with a bandsaw. Now I am able to use a digital drawing that is water-jet cut. The cost is about the same when you balance it with the amount of time it would have taken manually. This allows me to focus on the stimulating and fun parts and areas that make the product feel handmade, such as the handle.

Now we have worldwide orders there are no longer such pronounced seasonal spikes, which means we have a constant stream that is easier to manage and live from. The internet makes things much easier because you can search for good suppliers online, and you can also learn new skills from other people on YouTube, for example. Rather than compete with large online marketplaces, we are able to distinguish ourselves from them in terms of packaging and personalization, which people seem to favour. We try to provide a personal service where we can.

Success does also bring challenges. The more popular you are the more emails and phone calls you receive, which takes away from the time you can spend making; sometimes you can't physically stop what you are doing to answer the phone, which is why I now have Bluetooth headphones that allow me to answer the phone while quenching hot steel.

It is important to point out that most craftspeople don't have a pension plan, and I know that in ten years' time my elbows and hands won't be the same. It's good to keep this in mind and prepare to look at alternatives, whether this is finding more ways you can acquire mechanical help with parts of the process or whether you could take on an apprentice.

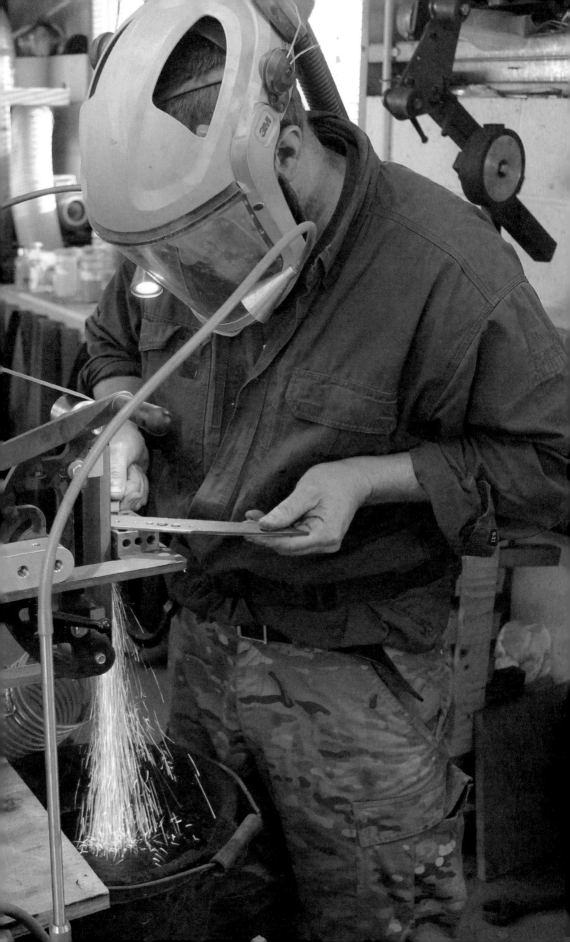

CONSERVING THE CRAFT AND ITS LIVELIHOOD

I'm passionate about making things, which means I'm passionate about talking about them. I want to share what I know with other people and spread the enjoyment and satisfaction I get from it. Some people believe that by passing on our knowledge we are encouraging people to simply make their own tools, especially at a time when being resourceful and self-sufficient is extremely popular. While this is true to an extent, I don't think this is as damaging as some think it is: I make knives, but I also like to buy knives. I can appreciate other people's work because I know what went into it. I enjoy looking at, critiquing, and learning from what someone else has created. There are always people who go hunting, fishing, and enjoy green woodworking, and will therefore need a tool.

Through demonstrations at shows and online platforms such as YouTube, we are educating people on how to make our product. I get a huge amount of satisfaction from inspiring others. The great thing about crafts is that they appeal to such a wide audience – we have toddlers and great grandfathers alike watching our process at shows. We love helping other people find the same kind of happiness and enjoyment we have. For example, teaching a child who is not doing well at school how to make things and see them find their niche in life is incredible. I am still learning every day and I am happy to continue passing on this learning to other people and keep the craft alive.

AXE MAKING

Dating from the stone age, the axe is one of the most basic and hardest working of tools used in various situations to cut through wood, rock, ice, and metal. At first, they were simply a handheld head, but later a handle of bone or wood was added, and the material of the axe head changed from stone to metal. The axe has been used as a tool, but also as a weapon and even a ceremonial object. The basic design has not changed since around 1200 BCE, but the craftsmanship required to make one has evolved, resulting in a tool that is still used and valued today.

"Looking into the ways in which black-smiths used to work is like time-travel. Basically, I use the same techniques as smiths have been using through the ages, but I have the privilege of both their knowledge and the ability to combine that with modern resources"

John Neeman

JOHN NEEMAN

Priekuļi, Latvia | autinetools.com

Training: Self-taught

Located next to the family home, John's business – Autine Tools – operates from a spacious workshop that houses a team of five, including his sister and brother. By learning how to delegate, and with the help of social media for marketing, John has balanced his time allowing him time to develop his designs and skills while focusing on the well-being of both himself and his team.

ORIGINS

Since I was a child, I have always been curious about what things are and how they are made. This led to me exploring the nature around my parent's farmhouse and in particular exploring my father's tool shed. I loved being in the forest and going fishing, where it is essential to carry a good knife with you. As I could not afford a knife for myself, I started wondering if I could make one. Slowly, I gathered some necessary tools, and a neighbour gifted me my first anvil, which had been sitting unused in her barn. By burning wood to make charcoal, I turned the family's old barn into a forge where I would spend many hours experimenting with tools and materials, learning from any book available, and searching for information online.

With my first success – making a chisel out of an old truck spring – it felt as if I was doing something right. I had found the joy of creating and have had it ever since. Fortunately, there were many people looking for well-crafted tools and my hobby quickly turned into a full-time job.

MOTIVATIONS

When creating, I feel fantastic. It is as if I am playing, combining shapes and materials, and making a bit of magic using fire, wood, steel, and leather. I enjoy every moment of this game, like a child! Of course, as soon as this game became my job, I had orders to be made on time as people waited for their tools. It sometimes feels like an obligation; the work becomes monotonous. Then I remind myself that I do what I like and can make a living out of it. In my opinion, this is the way our world should function.

"Being a craftsman is not an easy lifestyle, but for me and my team our work is our well-being; it is our lifestyle"

I would say that interest in woodcraft and bushcraft has always been alive and always will be. It is just that nowadays, with social media and the ease of spreading information, craftsmen have become celebrities in their own way. It is fashionable to be a bushcrafter, making and using handmade things, even though it has always been a part of our lives; it just hasn't been as visible before now. From the local market place, craftsmen have made their way through websites and Instagram, which allow them to reach people worldwide. I think it is great! The sense of community between craftspeople has also benefited from the increased communication. We follow many toolmakers around the world, and it is common to share our latest creations with each other, as well as some tips and tricks (not all of them, obviously, because each expert has secrets that make their tools one of a kind). We will always have lots to talk about between ourselves. That is just the way we are – we live the craft and it is our favourite topic of discussion.

Looking into the ways in which blacksmiths used to work is like time-travel. Basically, I use the same techniques as smiths have been using through the ages, but I have the privilege of both their knowledge and the ability to combine that with modern resources. I have deep respect for what these people have given to humanity, researching and creating tools essential to survival. Being a craftsman is not an easy lifestyle, but for me and my team our work is our well-being; it is our lifestyle.

WORKSPACE AND TOOLS

My forge is located in a hundred-year-old barn next to my family home. We are privileged to have a beautiful view over Rauna river valley from our windows and are surrounded with peace and quiet. Fortunately, we have a spacious workshop with plenty of room for inspiration, creativity, and work.

Over the years I have gathered many tools for my forge to make work as efficient and comfortable as possible, but what is essential for a workspace like ours is safety – one of our main considerations. We basically use the same tools blacksmiths have used for centuries: an anvil, a forge, and a hammer. We also work with drills, a bandsaw, a grinding machine and, of course, a power hammer, which is used to forge the shape of the axe head. I found my power hammer in a landfill and traded it for a knife I made. I restored it and it has been a great help ever since. Some may say that the power hammer is not authentic to heritage arts. I say that if smiths back in the day had the opportunity to use it, they would. Instead, they had apprentices to swing the heavy hammers while their master held the tool to be forged. I also consider my own health, as the power hammer makes my work a little safer.

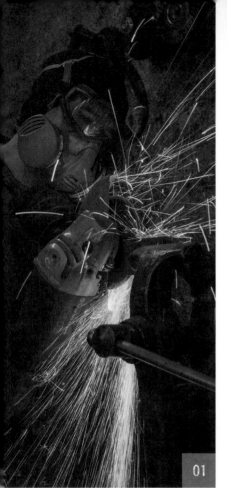

PROCESS OVERVIEW

01 We start by cutting steel billets (bars of metal that are used as a starting point in metalwork) made at the right size for each knife and axe. These are cut from larger billets using a hot chisel, angle grinder, machine saw, and hacksaw.

02 The main shape of the axe is forged using a power hammer. At this stage we are using the weight and force from the hammer to shape the hot, now malleable steel billet.

03 Heat treatment is also an essential part of the forging process. Heating the steel up to the right temperature ensures the hardness of the blade will be just right – not too hard and brittle, nor too soft. We use a special oven that can be heated up to a maximum of 1500°C. Quenching the tool

in oil is part of the heat treatment and also gives the tools that beautiful black finish on them. When forging, the fewer times the steel needs to be heated, the better, as during heating it is exposed to oxygen at high temperatures, which might affect the durability of the steel later.

04 When it comes to shaping the details, a hammer and hand are used for precision. Different hand hammers, different tongues to hold the steel, and various tools we have created ourselves are used throughout the process. The ability to improvise in this part of forging is an important skill that a good smith should know how to use. Different chemicals are also involved to unite steels and to reveal the beautiful patterns of Damascus steel. It is therefore not only strong

hands that make a good smith; a knowledge of chemistry is also needed.

05 Once the forging is complete there is still lots to do – grinding the tools is a very special part of the process. We start grinding with rougher belts to remove the excessive steel and continue up with finer grinds to achieve a polished look and razor sharpness.

06 At Autine we make the tools from start to finish, meaning we not only make the steel parts, but also the handles and leather accessories. Currently our basic supply includes several wood and precious wood sorts for knife handles. Handles of axes are made from elm, which is one of toughest and hardest trees we have in Latvia.

The handles are created by carefully selecting the wood type best suited for the tool, cutting the rough shape with a bandsaw, and then grinding the shape out with a drawknife, carpenter's axe, belt grinder, and sand paper.

07 We use natural, thick cow skin for our sheaths to protect the blade from possible damage, and also to protect the user from damage that the blade might cause. We cut out the shape required from a sheet of leather. The leather is then stitched with a waxed thread and fit to the tool individually. We use natural dyes to add colour to the sheaths and use a beeswax-based treatment to smooth the leather and make it durable.

FORGING A CAREER

In my opinion, blacksmithing, or bladesmithing as I love to call my job, is a profession that will be relevant for humanity no matter how far technology progresses. Man's most reliable tools are his hands, and as long as there are people who appreciate handmade craft, smiths will have work to do. I am dedicated to doing my work as well as I can, and to improving my skills with every axe or knife I make. I take responsibility for each one of the tools that comes out of my forge, and people appreciate that. It is important to maintain a good reputation to continue doing my job.

After I started selling my first tools, I quickly realized that I cannot do everything alone. If I keep having to answer the phone and emails, I cannot give myself a hundred per cent to forging. I am lucky to have my family – my brother Matiss and sister Karline – to help with the leather craft and organize supplies, shipments, bookkeeping, and communication with clients. Everyone does what they are best at, concentrating on one thing at a time to produce the finest result.

Luckily, we now have work all year round. As much as we would like to, we do not go to craft shows and markets because there is no time. We sell mostly online and promoting our tools on social media is effective enough. These days it feels good to wake up and know there is work to do. I go to my forge, check my list of orders, and get to work – heating up the forge, preparing materials, heating the steel, and forging and shaping it. I love the sound of hot steel cooling in oil. If there are no urgent orders, I enjoy sketching new designs for tools or taking my bow outside to practise my shooting skills. Planning your own day is a privilege a self-employed craftsman can enjoy.

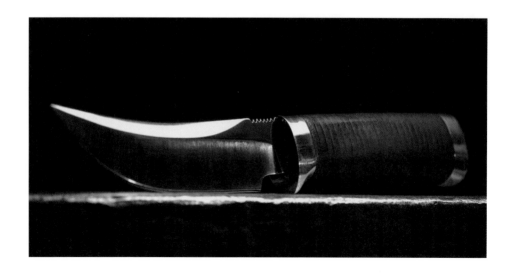

SURVIVING IN THE MODERN WORLD

Modern society is accustomed to having everything created and supplied instantly. It can be hard for people to understand that our pace is as fast as it can be; it takes time to make a tool with the maximum amount of care and attention given to every single detail. When a craft becomes your business, it is difficult to find the time to fulfil orders as well as make time for creativity and experimentation, but we try hard to find the best balance between the two. It is important to delegate duties, and as there is such a high demand for the tools I make, I decided to teach apprentices. We now have a total of five people on the team.

"I have people helping me to create my social media content; I can forge an excellent axe, but I can't film an exciting video!"

Social media has had the biggest impact on my decision to progress my hobby into a business. It is an essential selling tool for craftspeople who want to reach out to a worldwide audience. Latvia is a small country and with a population of barely two million, and few good blade makers, our target audience there can have its limits. We started by posting YouTube videos and Facebook photos that went viral, and now also have an Instagram account with a following of over twenty-four thousand. We feature daily sneak peeks into our forge and finished items. I have people helping me to create my social media content; I can forge an excellent axe, but I can't film an exciting video!

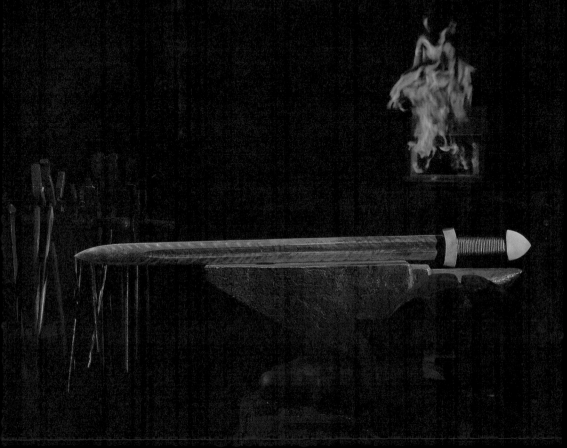

CONSERVING THE CRAFT AND ITS LIVELIHOOD

We believe that craft is not to be kept to yourself – if you practise a craft, it should be passed on. If we live and study the craftsmanship, it will survive. The world as we know it, with humans, cannot exist without craft.

By not only using the methods our ancestors used, but also improving them, we share the craft. There are, of course, innovations that help us to make tools with more speed and ease, more precisely and more safely. We still do everything the "traditional way", as modern tools only help us rather than do the job for us. That is the real value of craftsmanship – the touch of the expert's hand that cannot be felt in mass-produced items.

I am mostly self-taught, learning the craft on my own. I have never been an apprentice to any smith, nor have I wished to be one. In some ways, one must be self-taught to create truly original work with their unique signature. In my own experience, teachers tend to give too much information to their students, trying to show them what is right and wrong. But to be creative, there must be space for imagination. Of course, passing on knowledge and techniques is important – they must not be lost. I can share my own story and knowledge, but each person must create their own tale to become a true master of their craft. I feel like the luckiest man in the world to be able to do what I love, to express myself in my creations, and to even earn a living while doing it. What else is there to wish for?

WOODWORKING

As you will see in this book, woodworking can take many forms and use a variety of different tools. Many crafters maintain the purity of traditional, handcrafted tools while others incorporate modern-day machinery into long-established workflows. What they all have in common is an adoration for the material they work with and a devotion to celebrating its natural properties.

"Nothing beats having the time to appreciate all of your five senses working together at once... Minutes turn into days in the blink of an eye when you are in a state of mindful making"

EJ Osborne

EJ OSBORNE

Somerset, UK | www.hatchetandbear.co.uk

Training: Product & Furniture Design at Kingston University + Arboriculture
with the Royal Forestry Society + Self-taught

EJ Osborne, founder of Hatchet+Bear, is a designer-woodworker who creates a wide range of functional utensils and tools for everyday use, including chopping and serving boards, knives, spoons, spatulas, combs, and handloom kits. His experience in both design and green woodworking gives him a distinct edge in the craft business that is testified by the quality and originality of his products. With the success of the Hatchet+Bear brand, EJ runs his own courses, sells his products in an online shop, wrote a book on spoon carving, and has made multiple television appearances as both a craft expert and a presenter.

ORIGINS

It is quite hard to pin a starting point for my experience of craft. I would say I have always been a maker of things and as I grow, the things I choose to make often change – it's just one long journey that I love being on. I was always drawing and inventing things as a child and in my twenties, living and working in London, I would often indulge in ambitious and sometimes hideous DIY projects in the rented and shared houses I lived in. One thing that has always been a constant is my material choice: my love for trees and their timber.

When I left university, I wanted only two things: to work with wood and for life to be simple. A few years later, I left London to go and live that simpler life – in Somerset. Within a few months, I had a calling to carve a wooden spoon. It seemed to make perfect sense. I was living somewhere surrounded by vast woodland in which I walked and spent most of my days, and I only needed a few hand tools to start. I became smitten with carving freshly foraged green wood. I carved spoons and then other wooden utensils all day and sometimes all night, and it was not long before people were asking to buy them. From those small beginnings sprung a wealth of woody ideas and now I make all sorts of items. I call myself a designer-woodworker.

MOTIVATIONS

Working with wood I have searched for and collected straight from the tree and using my hand tools to carve it is one of the most enjoyable – and most important – things about my craft. I like that it is a hundred times slower than going to buy timber from a shop and using machine tools. It is slow making at its best; mindful woodworking. There is time to consider everything – whether it is about the design of what you are making or just pondering life. Nothing beats having the time to appreciate all of your five senses working together at once – the scent of freshly cut wood as you slowly shave lengths of bark to the ground with a razor-sharp knife, the sound of your axe chopping and slicing through the fresh succulent flesh of freshly fallen branches. Minutes turn into days in the blink of an eye when you are in a state of mindful making.

"I think there is enormous value in the experience of engaging in a slow craft – mental well-being is at the top of the list"

There has been a massive rise in the popularity of traditional crafts over the past few years – both people engaging in crafts and people wanting to buy craft products; and then under the craft umbrella there has been a huge increase in people engaging in woodwork – even more specifically, green woodwork or carving fresh wood. I think there is enormous value in the experience of engaging in a slow craft – mental well-being is at the top of the list. People who are buying craft items are yearning to own things that have that undeniable feeling, that tactile nature of being been made by hand, in a world where most things are now not.

The great thing with any movement is that it creates a sense of community. Green woodworking's rise in popularity has really exploded online. With an abundance of social media groups, trending hashtags, high-profile Instagram accounts, and busy YouTube channels, there is a lot to tap into on the subject and it has now become easier than ever to talk with other woodworkers, to learn new skills and be inspired.

I think it is important to understand the history of one's craft. I am certainly inspired and impressed by the roots of green woodworking – especially in its medieval era. That was a significant time for green woodwork. Most of the methodology remains the same and I love this. If it isn't broken, don't fix it. When you only have to use a few uncomplicated hand tools to get the job done and that job has been around since the middle ages, you know that you are probably not going to be able to design those tools any better. Green wood as a material has its limitations and we would once use it to make many more products than we do today. The modern world of mass manufacture has largely taken over – but I like to disrupt that theory and I love the challenge of helping people to choose a wooden product over a plastic one.

WORKSPACE AND TOOLS

As I expanded and started to make a broader range of wooden things, my toolkit grew and so did the need for a bigger space. I am currently on my third workshop. All of them I have loved for different reasons. The first was the living room in our house – that's where it all started as a business. When I realized I was finding woodchips in the bedroom, I knew it was time to upsize. Then there was a barn on a farm – that was freezing but its sheer size and the idea of being able to make larger things was very exciting.

Now I am here – in the middle of a field and some trees sits a brick-built workshop and office. The workshop has two large up-and-over doors, ensuring I can roll in a tree if I need to; the large office space means I can use a computer and a printer without both being covered in woodchip or dust (although I would prefer to stare out of the window at the trees than use the computer).

I don't tend to have anything in either the office or the workshop that I would not use – by nature, large pieces of tree propped up against the walls and a row of axes make the place look great. More importantly they are the things that fill me with joy when I walk in of a morning.

The tools I mainly use are a chainsaw to saw sections of tree, a handsaw and an axe to further form and roughly cut shapes, and a knife to shape and finish things. Obviously with growing demand and higher output I could not be without the help of a machine or two, and I do a lot of cutting with a bandsaw. It is vintage; I called it Simon. I also I have a planing machine, which cuts all the plank-wood smooth, and a belt sander. In spite of these additions, my workshop is quite low-tech compared to a lot of woodworkers with a similar output. I like it this way and have set a limit on the amount of equipment present in my workshop.

PROCESS OVERVIEW

01 I spend time in the woods looking for suitable trees to either fell or prune – although sometimes a tree surgeon will contact me to say they have cut down a roadside tree and ask me if I would like to take it. Most of the wood I use comes from old trees that are near the end of their life, trees felled to thin out woodland as part of a management programme, or storm-damaged roadside trees. Pruning or felling the wood is carried out using a chainsaw.

02 After the tree has been felled, a tree surgeon or I myself will cut off all the small branches and send them to be chipped or charcoaled, before I cut all the big branches off. I take a branch and have it sliced into planks on a large bed saw called a miser as and when I need material. Image 02 shows a large branch of English walnut before it is taken to be pinked on the miser.

03 To make chopping boards, as an example, I cut a plank into various lengths on the bandsaw. Depending on the type of chopping boards I am making, I then add some shape to each of the lengths. If the board requires a hanging hole or handle, I will drill or cut this at this stage. This will be my chopping board blank.

04 The blank is then sent through the planer on each side. This planes off the

surface of each flat side of the board, where any saw marks reside, eventually leaving them smooth and clean. Sometimes it is necessary to feed the board through several times to achieve a good result.

05 At this stage of the process, the sides and the sharp edges need sanding. Again there will be a rough surface to the edges – as a result of the initial cutting and shaping – but with some time moving slowly on the sanding belt, they soon grind down and become smooth to the touch. I adopt a similar technique to remove the sharp edges all the way round, ensuring the whole board is a pleasure to handle and to look at.

06 Oiling is the final stage and one of my favourite tasks. It not only nourishes, conditions, and protects the wooden board, but it also brings out the vibrancy within the wood, highlighting its colour and grain. I use a soft cloth to apply a generous slathering of flaxseed oil all over the board. The board is left for a couple of hours to fully absorb the oil before I wipe the excess off. The board is now complete.

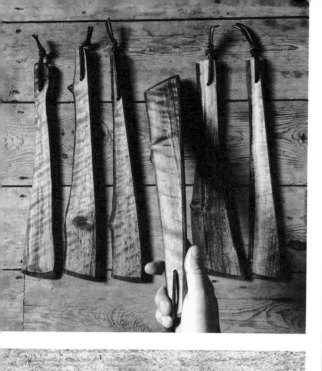

FORGING A CAREER

Like most craftspeople I know, it took me some time to find my feet in terms of developing what I loved doing into an actual business that pays me enough to live on. It can be quite financially tough in the beginning, which is why it is such a bonus to have a low start-up cost. The first place I started to sell my utensils was the local market. Shortly after, I set up an online shop and soon realized that with the help of building a social media following I could make the two work together really well. This meant I didn't need to spend my time working on the stall any more, although some craftspeople really thrive on the real-world environment of a market – the meeting of customers and them being able to touch the products.

I have not yet engaged in any shows or exhibitions because I have been busy pursuing other avenues that enable me to promote my work in new and exciting ways. I teach people how to carve their own wooden utensils through my *Weekend in the Woods* courses, which are held in the middle of the wood around the campfire. I wrote my first book on one area of my craft, which was published at the beginning of 2017, and I have also supplied and stocked in various shops. At the end of 2017, I was asked to audition as a BBC television presenter within my field after producers had seen my Instagram profile and online shop. Publishers and producers of books, magazines, and TV shows are always looking for something unique or even something really simple but executed in an audience-capturing way, which is I think why I was approached to write my book and do work for the BBC. My biggest piece of advice would be to say yes to everything you like the sound of and believe in yourself – and then keep going. All of these things have raised my profile and in turn boosted visitors to my online shop.

I never really thought about other streams of income when I started out on social media. All I wanted to do was show people what I was doing. I am a very keen photographer and writer, so when I have finished making products, I like to spend a lot of time styling and photographing them before finding the words to explain them. Great photographs and thoughtful words coupled with hard work, determination, and a relentless belief in what I am making have been the winning formula to success so far. I also found that investing my energy online gave me an extremely wide audience and as a result I have customers all over the world. When you put a few words down to go with the photographs you post on Instagram, and you are consistent with this process, you begin to find your unique voice. I think people become really interested in the whole picture of *you* and what *you* are doing.

I don't plan what to make too far ahead, unless I have an order to fulfil; I like to wake up and be free to make whatever I feel like. I am a bit of a creative meanderer and I think this works in harmony with being a woodland wanderer! I think running my own craft business will always be hard work but it is perfectly balanced by the fact that I get to do what I love to do. I eat, sleep, and breathe Hatchet+Bear. We have become one entity.

SURVIVING IN THE MODERN WORLD

There are not enough hours in the day to make everything I would like to make right at that moment. And some of my ideas are not quite fully formulated – or perhaps I feel like the world isn't quite ready for them yet. I therefore write absolutely every idea down – the moment I have the thought – on a scrap of paper. I have bits of paper going back years, but every now and then I will shuffle through and bring one idea to the top and start working on it. This has always been my method and even if I stopped jotting ideas down now, I would already have enough to last me a lifetime.

The one thing that is definitely not constant is the world around me and its trends. I look at the many things that are always going on in other design disciplines to pick up on trends that I can apply to my woodwork – for example, design movements experiencing a resurgence, the latest colour and pattern trends, seasonal shifts, fashion, graphic design, and interior design and architecture. I will look at anything and if I think it in some way would work well in my world of wood, then I make it happen.

Partly for this reason, I tend to make test batches of things. Ten is my favourite number to work to. Everything is a bit of a gamble, but generally I have a feel for what my customers like, so I am usually confident that things will sell. If they do, I make more and the item will become a staple in the online shop. It is a feel-your-way-around approach that keeps me incredibly connected with what is happening, creates minimal wood waste, and keeps me on my toes.

Obviously, I have to constantly adapt my work schedule and divide my time between the various arms of Hatchet+Bear that I have created. I never wanted to be exclusively in the physical making of things; I think people often have the idea that growth of a business is only measured by product output. I wanted my craft to be so much more than that. For me, the products are just one part. The teaching, writing, photography, and TV presenting are all just as important in creating the whole picture of what I am trying to say to the world with my craft.

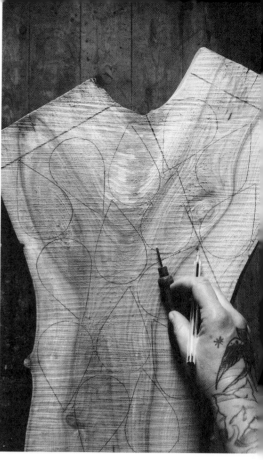

CONSERVING THE CRAFT AND ITS LIVELIHOOD

It is so important to conserve craft skills. With regard to my personal journey into the field of green woodworking, I would never have known about any of it, nor would I have been able to engage with it, had it not been for those who had been before me who took the time to record, communicate, and pass on their knowledge of traditional and heritage skills. It is my hope as a designer and maker that the advancements I have made, my work, and my thoughts will go on to help push the boundaries, expanding yet again on those solid foundations. I want to ensure the generations ahead of me can use what I have left behind and, indeed, expand upon it again.

We absolutely cannot allow everything we do by hand to be lost to those things being done by machine. It is my belief that the making of things by hand is one of the core elements of being human – the act of engaging in craft brings all of your senses into play. What is the point of our existence if we no longer need to see, smell, hear, taste, or touch?

SPOON CARVING

As a creative process that can be enjoyed with hand tools alone in your living room at night, spoon carving is certainly a very accessible craft that can be a great starter for anyone looking to take their first steps into green woodworking. There is beauty in something that on the surface can seem so simple yet when examined with more discerning eyes reveals an almost magical union of natural material and human industry.

"Each spoon is a little sculpture, a very complex three-dimensional shape to carve, with many variables. Yet it has a very specific purpose to fulfil"

Éamonn O'Sullivan

ÉAMONN O'SULLIVAN

County Mayo, Ireland | hewn.ie

Training: Self-taught

Éamonn and his business, Hewn, epitomize the importance of brand development for anyone looking to carve a place for themselves as a professional craftsperson. Exquisitely formed and elegantly photographed, Éamonn's spoons are created with a genuine admiration for their function and purpose.

ORIGINS

Growing up on the west coast of Ireland, I did lots of outdoor things but I have always been quite academic too. I followed a fairly normal route through the education system to university in Galway, and straight into a job as a consultant ecologist. I was introduced to the idea of spoon carving by a friend of the family and soon after, during a period of unemployment, I took a deep dive into traditional woodworking. I must have watched hundreds of hours of videos (I always say I have an unaccredited degree from the University of YouTube) and read many books, all about green woodworking, seventeenth- and eighteenth-century woodworking, and traditional woodland management. I have a BSc in Environmental Science; spoon making is quite a shift but my degree covered certain topics that are very useful to me in my craft, including botany, wood anatomy, tree taxonomy, and woodland management.

I bought many second-hand and new tools. I learned to make stools, bowls, baskets, and other things, but I really took to carving spoons. About a year later, I left my full-time job as an ecologist and set up my spoon-carving business, Hewn. It seems like an unusual move to make, to leave a good job that I was interested in and could have made a good living at. Some people around me certainly saw it that way; but I think I just wanted to make things for a living and decided to do it before I was too grown up to take a risk.

MOTIVATIONS

Spoons are intensely interesting to me. Unlike the fork, for instance, spoons have been in common use since pre-history. A spoon is a basic, fundamental tool, used several times a day, to feed you. It is one of the most intimate objects people own. It literally enters the body! It has to feel right in the hand and in the mouth. Hence, there are many things to get right. A truly good spoon is a delight to use. Using wooden eating spoons in particular is a joy that most people miss out on.

Each spoon is a little sculpture, a very complex three-dimensional shape to carve, with many variables. Yet it has a very specific purpose to fulfil. It may seem limiting to work within such strict confines, but somehow I find that there is more than enough room for creativity and inspiration. I think the challenge of making a spoon that not only works very well but is also beautiful, characterful, and robust, is what fascinates me and keeps my focus on this object. I will probably never make the perfect spoon and that is what keeps me trying.

> "It may seem limiting to work within such strict confines, but somehow I find that there is more than enough room for creativity and inspiration"

There has been a renaissance of the heritage crafts. The very existence of this book and the popularity of other books on similar topics prove it. I think people are losing interest in bland, mass-produced items in favour of the character, personality, and known provenance of the handmade. Such things cost more but they are more meaningful, more enjoyable, and often better quality. In addition to that, many people are taking up spoon making and other crafts as hobbies, maybe in search of that satisfaction of creation that they don't get at their regular jobs.

I think all humans have a drive to be useful, to create or do something that has a positive effect on others. It's very satisfying to make a functional object. Making something useful needs no explanation or justification. I just make spoons for people to use. The sheer simplicity of that is very enjoyable. I love to reflect on the fact that there are thousands of my spoons out there being used and (hopefully) enjoyed every day. It is worth considering that perhaps some of those afflicted by depression or malaise have found themselves in an occupation that doesn't seem useful to them, or because its usefulness is so indirect or obscure that it is difficult to understand.

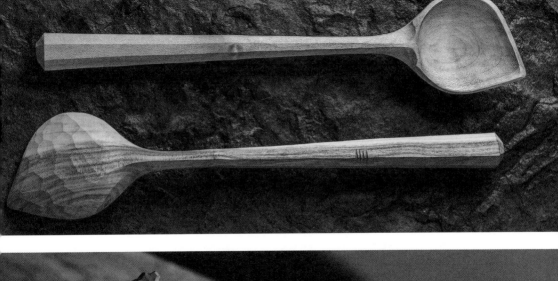

WORKSPACE AND TOOLS

I was lucky in that I was able to use an existing wooden-framed outbuilding on my property as my workspace when I started out. It was, however, totally cluttered and unfinished at the time. Having realized the importance of an uncluttered workshop, I have since tried to clear away everything that I don't need on a day-to-day basis. It can be difficult to focus sometimes and your workspace should facilitate clear thinking and an easy workflow rather than hinder it. It should be as clean and tidy as possible, not that I always succeed in following that particular dictate. But every time I have invested time and effort into improving or cleaning my workspace, I have wondered why I didn't do it sooner.

My most important tools are my axe, knives, and sharpening stones. Without the latter, the rest are useless since all edge tools, no matter the quality, need regular sharpening to work correctly. Sharpening is probably the most useful skill that everybody has forgotten. The axe is used for cleaving and chopping the wood into a rough spoon shape. A straight knife is used to refine and finish the spoon shape, and a bent knife, or "spoon knife", is used to hollow out the bowl. A spoon can be made with these tools alone but a number of other tools help to speed up the process, including a chainsaw, froe and wedges, mallet, carving block, shaving horse, and drawknife.

PROCESS OVERVIEW

01 I start at the woodpile by selecting a suitable piece of green wood. This will depend on the type of spoon I wish to make. For instance, certain spoon designs require a suitable bend or crook. The key to a strong spoon is in keeping the wood fibres as long as possible, that is, matching the shape of the wood to the shape of the piece.

02 I cleave the wood into two halves, through the pith (the centre of the tree), using a froe or an axe. Crucially, the split will follow the grain of the wood. The pith will be visible, as a darker line down the middle of the cleft face. Usually, each half will become a spoon. In larger diameter wood, I may continue cleaving into several smaller, spoon-sized billets.

03 I begin carving with the axe, removing the pith and establishing the crank (the angle between the handle and the bowl). This angle is critical to a well-functioning spoon.

04 I now have a surface onto which I can draw my spoon shape. I may use a template or draw it freehand, making sure the spoon is positioned so that it takes advantage of the natural shape of the wood, for maximum strength.

05 I remove all the wood that is not a spoon, until I end up with a "spoon blank", a crudely spoon-shaped block, to be refined with knives later. This kind of rapid stock removal is the axe's strong suit. I start by cutting to my lines, on both

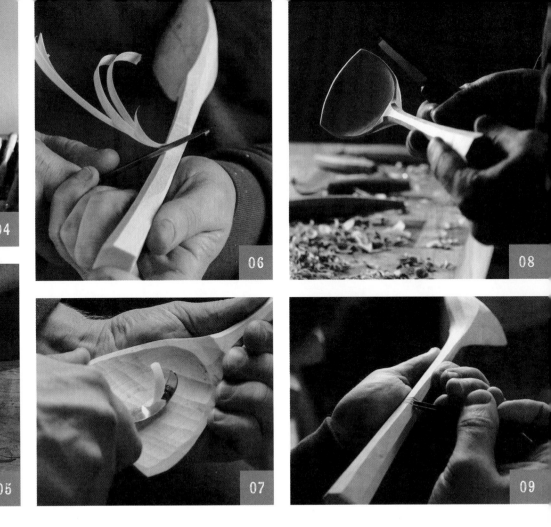

sides of the spoon, before roughly shaping the back/underside of the spoon.

06 The shape of the spoon blank is refined using a straight knife. This phase takes the most time. It is where the spoon takes its final shape. The moisture in green wood makes it softer and easy to carve. I try to create long, clean lines and avoid very sharp edges that will wear quickly in use.

07 The bowl is hollowed last, using a spoon knife, which is a single-bevel bent knife. The majority of the hollowing is done by cutting across the grain. The shape and finish of the spoon's bowl and its rim are particularly important to a well-functioning eating spoon.

08 When I am happy with the spoon's shape, I leave it for a few days to dry before making the finishing cuts. Wood hardens as it dries. Smoother, shiny finishing cuts can be achieved in dry wood, with a freshly sharpened knife. I do not sand my spoons. Sanding is boring, time-consuming and, if not done extremely carefully, rounds over the crisp, hand-cut facets. It can also lead to "fuzziness" after washing.

09 I sign my spoons with my mark and soak them in a warm solution of linseed oil and a small amount of beeswax. While oiling is not strictly necessary, it does bring out the contrast in the grain and offers some protection against the rigours of constant washing.

FORGING A CAREER

When I began considering making a living from spoon carving, I was not at all sure that I could do it. There is no getting around the fact that it is difficult to make profit from crafts, which are generally very labour intensive. One of the most common pitfalls I have noticed is under-pricing. Existing in the market alongside endless cheap, mass-produced items is no easy task, especially in the first few years of establishing yourself, when any new business struggles. So establishing a career in handcraft, particularly, is a fine balancing act. It is hard to know if there is enough demand for your work and, furthermore, nobody starts off as a great master. It takes thousands of hours of practice to become proficient, so the first few years are a mixture of creating and establishing good branding and building your own skills to live up to the high quality of the brand.

I have noticed that many modern makers initially have other ways of making money that are flexible enough to allow them to develop their craft without risking too much financially. I was no exception and I think that is a sensible way to get started. I will say though that at some point you have to commit and have the conviction that you are good enough to make things that people will want. It takes confidence.

"It is easier than ever for makers to sell directly to consumers at a reasonable price without handing over a chunk to a middle man"

As I learned about pricing and retailing, I quickly realized how little of what is spent in a retail shop actually goes into the making of the object. It is a tiny percentage. The internet is the greatest gift to heritage crafts. It allows people like me to connect directly to their customers. Thanks to the internet, I can carry on a business that is so labour intensive and "unscalable" that it would make a business advisor cry. It is not a classic, profit-driven business yet it works very well for me. It is easier than ever for makers to sell directly to consumers at a reasonable price without handing over a chunk to a middle man. At the same time, consumers can easily support small makers and get more out of their purchase, emotionally, since they can deal with the maker himself. Almost all of my sales are online.

SURVIVING IN THE MODERN WORLD

In addition to making sure that everything that leaves your workshop is as good as you can make it, the best piece of advice I can offer is to buy a camera and learn to take photographs. The internet is your best friend and the internet likes photographs and videos. If you can't take beautiful photographs, you will probably struggle. The good news is that cameras are cheap these days and the internet is full of photography tutorials. Creating and running your own, top-class website is easy now too. The days of paying someone large amounts of money to design a website, for it only to become neglected and stale within a year, are thankfully long gone.

Managing my social media accounts and website is an essential part of my work. I devote some time every day to take and edit photographs and post them online. The time that takes is more than worth it for the advantage of having a regular dialogue with my customers and allowing them into the workshop, digitally, so to speak. As well as that, I am very inspired and encouraged by all the other makers I come across on Instagram, for instance. The constant stream of new ideas, feedback, discussions, and collaborations online keep driving me forward.

Time is my biggest constraint. I often find it hard to keep up with orders yet I don't want to make my products so expensive that they become rare luxury goods for the rich, more so than they already are. I am not interested in traditional processes only for nostalgia's sake or for posterity. Unlike some, to whom use of machinery of any kind is anathema, I use machines such as the bandsaw for parts of certain designs, in order to speed up production and reduce bodily wear and tear a little. Even so, many of my designs are no quicker or easier to make with a machine's help, so they are carved entirely with hand tools. No matter what, everything is finished with knives. I can relate to the purists to a degree because there are many pitfalls to using machines without the knowledge of how to do it traditionally. For years, I have made a living using just an axe and knives and only now, having developed a clear understanding of cleaving, spoon design, and the inherent qualities of wood, have I adopted machines for certain things.

CONSERVING THE CRAFT AND ITS LIVELIHOOD

I do what I do because of the generosity of others who shared their knowledge freely and I am more than happy to do the same. I am glad that spoon carving and other heritage crafts are growing. I want to continue living in a world where there is an alternative to mass-produced commodities from huge online retailers. It is not that I don't admire engineers and scientists, but I do hope that my children will feel that craft is an option for them if they wish. I run regular spoon-carving classes and really try hard to pass on everything I have learned. I am always excited to talk to people about spoon carving and woodworking in general; maybe they will find the same pleasure in making that I have.

In my most reflective, contemplative moments, I have wondered if my life is meaningful – if I could or should be making more effective, impactful use of my time. Perhaps the global capitalists are right – inexpensive, easily manufactured goods are the future. Perhaps crafts such as mine are a frivolous luxury. But I have bought many handmade objects from other people – spoons, baskets, tools, bags – and I love those things. I know that no one was taken advantage of to make them. I know where the materials came from. They function beautifully and are long lasting. I have an emotional connection to them so using them is a joy. I will treat them well and enjoy them until I die or wear them out. I admire the dedication and commitment it took to gain the skills and experience to make them. I know these things of myself but I am also lucky enough to receive many messages from people expressing similar feelings about my spoons, so I have to think that what I am doing is valuable.

WOODTURNING

Woodturning involves placing a wooden blank on a lathe, which then rotates the wood as the turner uses an additional tool to cut a shape from the wood. It is an age-old practice that can be traced back as far as ancient Egyptian times, where a two-person lathe was recorded. Since then lathes have developed into foot-powered pole lathes, which are still used today by green woodworkers. Modernity has also seen the introduction of electric power lathes. You will see the use of both types in this section.

"Turning and carving has become a very large part of my life, an expression of creativity that makes me happy and also fills my stomach and the fuel tank of my van"

Yoav Elkayam

YOAV ELKAYAM

Various locations, Europe | yoavkafets.bigcartel.com

Training: Self-taught + Course by Sharif Adams

Yoav Elkayam travels around Europe, living in a self-converted van: a big blue transporter with the faded printings of a moving company that reads "Pianos our speciality". Opening the big outer doors reveals a tiny home inside with its components made from wood in all its shapes: a kitchen, a bed, a bench, some baskets, a wood-burning stove – all simple, handmade, and created with attention to detail. The shelf on the wall holds several turned wooden bowls, plates, and mugs with a substantial collection of wooden spoons hanging underneath on a specially made rack. What started as a curiosity for making became a passion and a way of life. Yoav sells his products and teaches spoon carving and bowl turning in different parts of the world.

ORIGINS

How does a young man, born and raised in Israel, where his closest contact to wood was perhaps the avocado tree he planted in the backyard, get to actively keep up the traditional craft of bowl turning? Looking back on my origins, I was never really exposed to handcraft. It was as a musician, touring in the UK, that I saw handcrafted wooden products for the first time. It was during this period I got to know people who worked with green wood and created with their hands.

Several years ago, I found myself on a shaving horse with a drawknife, helping a friend to shape poles for a yurt he was building. With that simple experience came a new discovery: the outdoors – being in the woods, in the quiet, with no electricity, and only the sounds of birds singing on a tree close by. Later that evening the same friend handed me a knife, asking lightly if I would like to try to carve a spoon. In a way, I think I am still trying. Seeing this way of working really opened my eyes and pulled me to my current path. I searched the internet and followed the postings of green woodworkers, and slowly gained a feel and realization of what this craft could offer.

Back in Israel, I bought my first set of carving tools, made by Ben Orford (meet Ben on page 42), who encouraged me to explore green woodwork. This new inspiration also led me to building my own yurt, creating a space and a home for myself while avoiding the financial burden of living in rented accommodation. After attending a two-day bowl-turning and tool-forging course in the UK, I built my first pole lathe. Since then I have continued to turn and carve while improving my skills.

MOTIVATIONS

I remember how my first bowls all had holes in the bottom. Turning felt very unfamiliar and difficult in the beginning, but it just made me curious and eager to continue. And so I did, fascinated by how a foot-powered lathe, in a modern world of machines and engines, can still find its place and fit the pace I was looking for.

The possibility of working outside in nature, slow and silent, physical and creative, is what motivates me and inspires me most. I am still amazed by the fact that my workspace is a quiet outdoor space, rather than a closed, noisy workshop. Not needing to wear protective gear and avoiding the dust problems you would have in a confined space are a couple more of the advantages to working on this "old" and simple form of lathe, using hand tools and green woodworking methods.

I see pole-lathe-turning as a full-body experience, with a significant effect on my well-being, both physically and mentally. The work acts as a great mirror for me: there is no distinction between body, mind, and the item. If I am not focused or fully soaked from sweat in the process, it projects immediately on the product. I see the bowl or spoon as an excuse to actually experience the unlimited playground of making something with my own hands and spending time outdoors. Woodcraft is a field of self-empowerment for me, with spoons and bowls as brilliant by-products.

"I feel grateful for the chance to pass on the pleasure and empowerment of self-making that I experience myself as an everlasting student"

The growing community of craftspeople is clear. I feel part of a rising alternative of handcrafted culture led by more mindful makers, one that puts its focus on creating objects to be used in our daily lives. I literally put a lot of effort into creating useful objects, and as I am turning items, my aim is for them to be beautiful, long-lasting, and comfortable to use. Meeting and exchanging skills and experience with like-minded people through gatherings and online platforms is an important extension of and inspiration for my own work.

As part of this journey, I teach turning and spoon-carving courses. I feel grateful for the chance to pass on the pleasure and empowerment of self-making that I experience myself as an everlasting student. People spend a few days in nature, with the absence of daily stresses and constant white noise, sharing time together around an open fire under the stars and the trees, and they eventually discover the great potential of their own creativity. It can bring back a strong connection to nature and ourselves that I feel we tend to forget about.

WORKSPACE AND TOOLS

My home is the small space of nine square metres that contains everything I need and gives me shelter, mobility, and comfort. Moving between various corners of Europe, I am free to make wherever I like thanks to my current setup.

This is also where I store my tools. Everything has to fit into one storage box, so my toolkit is very basic. This limitation is especially positive as it means I only use what is really needed and keeps things as simple as possible. In the storage box lays a disassembled pole lathe that I can assemble anywhere. The rest of my toolkit consists of a small chopping block, a selection of hand-forged hook tools for bowl turning, an axe, and a couple of sloyd knives and hook knives for spoon carving and other small projects. The lathe is constructed from a log of ash, made into a bed (see diagram on page 314 for an example), with four tapered legs, a tool rest, two poppets, a bungee cord, two uprights (not always needed, it depends on the setup of your lathe), and a treadle.

Using a traditional pole lathe offers a useful benefit: the option of turning an item with an integrated projection, such as a handled mug or a spouted jug. These are items that are possible to fully turn on a pole lathe because of its reciprocating motion, meaning you can turn from one side of the projection and, with acquired control over the length of the spin with the foot treadle, stop on the other side of it. This allows the tool to cut on both sides of the handle or spout without breaking it off, something that would not be possible on an electric lathe, which constantly starts turning in one direction with the push of a button.

Wherever I am based I try to source a big log that will be used for the season for the turned items. Off-cuts, and also any branches or prunings that come along my way, will very likely be carved into spoons.

PROCESS OVERVIEW

01 Starting with a round log, I mark the length of a section needed to make a bowl. Using a spitting axe and wooden mallet, I split the log through its pith, releasing some of the tension in the wood. This reduces the chance of splits in the finished bowl when it dries.

02 Using a carving axe, I hew the top and bottom of the blank, keeping them parallel and creating a flat base. This also releases further tension from the wood. Using a pair of dividers, I find the middle point and score the circumference of the bowl.

03 I now axe out the rough shape of the bowl, trying to keep the blank even and balanced. This will help the spinning on the lathe later to be

as central as possible and result in a smoother process. I start from the base, making my way round and removing material, aiming towards the scribed line and desired shape.

04 After the axe work, I drill a hole in the centre of the bowl from the top and fit a mandrel in with the tap of a mallet. The mandrel is a cylindrical bit of wood that allows the treadle cord to run freely while the bowl is mounted on the lathe.

05 I can now mount the bowl on the lathe. Having a set centre on the mandrel and searching for the centre point on the base of the bowl, I make sure that it spins as central as possible. I then wrap the cord around the mandrel and secure the mounted bowl between the two lathe centres.

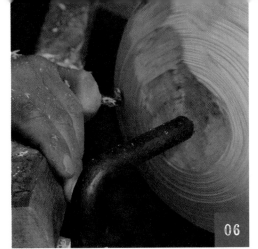

06 Turning, I start to shape the outside of the bowl with a hook tool, removing axe marks and slowly shaping the blank towards the desired form. This usually takes two to three passes on the full piece. After all the unwanted material is removed, I shape the bowl more carefully, starting from the base and making my way up to the rim.

07 Once I am happy with the form of the outer bowl, I take it off the lathe, flip it, and remount it, so that now the top surface faces me. Once again I start by cleaning all the axe marks on that face and evening the surface. I then hollow out the bowl. As I get deeper and thinner I constantly check the thickness of the wall and the depth with my fingers, aiming for a consistent wall thickness and a slightly thicker base.

08 When I reach the desired depth and inner shape I start undercutting the core of the bowl, where the mandrel is attached. By creating a cone and a weak point just above the base of the bowl, I can then easily break off the core to separate the mandrel from the bowl, leaving a small scar from the breakage. This core, if big enough, can be remounted again and be turned into a smaller bowl.

09 Once the bowl is off the lathe I clean the remains of the core at the base using a bent knife. The same is done on the foot of the bowl where it was mounted on the lathe. It will now sit to dry. Depending on the weather this might take between a week and a month. It is then oiled with raw linseed oil and ready to be used.

FORGING A CAREER

I don't recognize myself as a bowl turner; neither do I call it my "career". However, turning and carving has become a very large part of my life, an expression of creativity that makes me happy and also fills my stomach and the fuel tank of my van. There are periods in the year, especially in the summer season, when I find myself turning and making products for sale non-stop, for weeks or even months. Other times, I hardly produce and keep my time filled with other endeavours. For example, I purchased a bit of land with a couple of friends to form a quiet and creative living space and on which to grow our own food.

What fills my life now is a result of a continuous chain of meetings, incidents, and inspiration crossing my way, such as travelling with instruments and playing in festivals, seeing other people living in self-built, cosy mobile homes, and meeting green woodworkers. Apart from a bowl of porridge and coffee in the morning, my days are rarely predictable. I might work in the garden, help out some friends, read a book on a rainy day, or turn some bowls. I feel lucky to be able to choose how I shape my day-to-day life.

One thing leads to the other; my philosophy is that we should allow ourselves to fully encounter and engage with what we meet without binding ourselves to pre-made plans. This is how we understand how much life can offer. I therefore aim for days spent with meaningful activities. Green woodwork might be a long-lasting chapter but I keep in mind the organic evolution of life.

When I made a decision to try to make a living as a musician and then a craftsperson, I estimated how much money I could earn from that and then shaped my living structure accordingly. I decided to stop living in rented accommodation, to build a yurt instead, or later on to convert a van. Keeping my expenses low allows me to compromise less on how I make my income. This principle guides me still, just as the music that I play resonates in the wood I carve.

"Apart from a bowl of porridge and coffee in the morning, my days are rarely predictable... I feel lucky to be able to choose how I shape my day-to-day life"

SURVIVING IN THE MODERN WORLD

The modern world is neither an opponent to ancient handcraft nor does it replace it. It helps craftsmen and women to rise up through its media and connect globally. Taking my own story as an example, I grew up without any wood culture, but through seeing YouTube videos of bowl turners on the internet I became curious about what to me at that time was an unknown craft.

It is also due to the time we are living in that I don't need to be a son of a bowl turner to experience and access this craft. From my perspective as both a student and a teacher, this is a great advantage. The internet, whether I may like it or not, has become a supporting medium in making a living from what I produce and offers the opportunity to exchange knowledge and inspiration with others. Online platforms such as Instagram and an online shop help me to sell my products, sending them to different parts of the world wherever I am situated.

To some extent the appreciation and popularity of handcraft in society has decreased in modern times. The mass production of objects rolling from conveyer belts in huge factories is beyond comparison regarding accessibility and price. People still ask me how the manual production of bowls can efficiently sustain itself, as operating a machine by foot seems to be a symbol for slowness. But is it really? Is it actually the normal pace, the one that our own body provides and that we just tend to forget about inside the race of modern technology? In the twenty-first century people are used to upgrading their gadgets every month – a car of two years is considered old and inventions promise again and again new and improved efficiency. A big part of Western society is working on computers and communicating through phones, but never will it replace the natural desire to use all of our senses. Perhaps the well-rooted methods found in heritage crafts of working with our body and the materials around us in nature can provide this much-needed balance.

CONSERVING THE CRAFT AND ITS LIVELIHOOD

When friends come over to visit, I notice how nearly everyone, consciously or not, starts to play with the woodchips lying on the floor of my workspace. I believe we have a need to combine head and hand experiences, and that these have a powerful impact on us. As a tool, the pole lathe works surprisingly simply and allows anybody to operate it. At the same time, people have less and less need and opportunity to make something with their own hands, meaning that those who are courageous enough to try are initially confronted with a very steep learning curve. Some of the participants on the courses I run have never used an axe in their life, or cut a log with a handsaw, which means that even the first step of shaping the bowl blank with an axe might seem deceivingly simple but can in fact bring an almost insurmountable point of frustration or challenge.

Supporting people in overcoming this moment and helping them to continue increases confidence for the participant and is followed by a strong feeling of success for both of us. At the end of a course I watch the shining eyes of people holding a freshly turned bowl in their hands that will contain – for a long time – not only some food but also the memory and effort it took to make it.

If you have ever given a handmade gift to a friend as opposed to something you bought in a shop, you will know this difference. For me, the importance of crafting lays in the connection we make during the process of working with a wonderful material and transforming it into something beautiful and useful using our hands (not to mention the fact that trees are just incredible!). For this alone it is worth passing on this skill and I wish to make it accessible to as many people as possible.

FRANZ JOSEF KEILHOFER

Bavaria, Germany | gingerwood.de

Training: Self-taught

Franz Josef Keilhofer is a maker of a range of wooden products, including chopping boards, decorative wooden balls, and wine stoppers. Above all though he is a turner of wooden bowls of all shades and sizes. While most of his bowls are made from seasoned wood, a small percentage are made with green wood. As wood dries it starts to distort, so when working with unseasoned wood Franz allows the natural distortion to create beautifully unique items, almost acting as art pieces in their own right (see for example the bowl at the bottom of page 132). Supplementing his income with a variety of other activities means that Franz has found an ideal balance that allows him to live for the craft he loves.

ORIGINS

Born and raised on our family's farm in Bischofswiesen, a small village in the Bavarian Alps, I didn't plan to become a woodturner. I graduated from middle school and started an apprenticeship as a precision mechanic in plastic injection technology. After finishing my apprenticeship (*Gesellenbrief* in Germany, similar to a Bachelor's degree), I went back to college to get my A-levels. I then signed up at NAWI University in Salzburg to study science of engineering. Within my second semester I was diagnosed with severe depression and had to take a break from studying. This was when, by accident, I discovered woodturning. My activities were very limited due to my mental condition so I looked for a useful way in which to spend my time. I literally woke up one morning and thought: "Maybe I should start woodturning." I spent what money I had on a small lathe and built a woodturning shop in my garage. Although a short walk felt like climbing a mountain, spending time on my lathe never made me feel tired. It took me three years to overcome the worst part of my depression and woodturning was one of the things that kept me going. I became a self-employed woodturner two years after I bought my first lathe. I never took a class in woodturning and learned most things through trial and error.

MOTIVATIONS

One of the reasons I decided to start woodturning was that it is relatively cheap compared to other crafts. I found it affordable to invest in a small lathe, some tools, and everything else I needed to get started. Wood is also a beautiful material to work with. It can be a demanding lover, but once you internalize the basics you can form (and transform) it almost like a potter forms clay. I find great joy and satisfaction in creating timeless shapes inspired by what already exists inside a piece of wood. There is one ideal object hidden in every piece and I try to figure out what it looks like.

There has been an increase in people's awareness of woodcraft over the last few years, in part because there are more and more people working in an office job that they don't really like, living only for the weekend or the next vacation. Some of those people try to make woodworking a hobby or at least enjoy watching craftspeople in documentaries and dreaming about becoming a crafter themselves. There is a strong desire in most of us to create something with our own hands, something that lasts. Being a woodturner is hard, physical work but the kind of tiredness you get in the evening is a positive one. You know you have spent the day creating something that can last for generations. You are a maker of things and not an executer of tasks; you are only accountable to your own aims and creativity rather than working within somebody else's vision. I could not imagine working in a nine-to-five job ever again and I believe woodturning helps me to maintain my mental well-being.

"I find great joy and satisfaction in creating timeless shapes inspired by what already exists inside a piece of wood"

WORKSPACE AND TOOLS

I work in a modern workshop located on the family farm, right next to my showroom under my apartment. It is embedded in the mountains, surrounded by green fields and trees. I can proudly say that I work and live where others spend their vacation.

I am a messy person who doesn't like mess, so I am in constant conflict with myself. When I rebuilt my workshop from scratch two years ago, I tried to organize it as much as possible. Every tool has its place to make it easier for me to keep order or at least to make it easier to clean up after I have created a mess. It is not the cosy and quaint wooden cabin with dusty spider webs around that people have in mind when they think about a woodworking shop, but it helps me to stay focused. One of the best things about living on a farm is that we have all the heavy machinery available – like a tractor and a crane – that makes it easier to move heavy logs. Our barn provides a lot of space to store logs until they are processed. We have our own little forest, where I cut down trees by myself, but I prefer to go easy on my resources and buy trees from neighbours or the local authority, those that have already been cut down for good reasons.

My key tools are a chainsaw, bandsaw, an electric woodturning lathe, bowl gouge, and of course my hands.

PROCESS OVERVIEW

01 Filleting the log with a chainsaw and deciding about the placement of the future bowl in the context of the grain is possibly the most important step in the process, although of course every step is important. The goal is to get the most out of every log as well as to place the bowl in a way that ensures it will look as good as possible.

02 I then cut out a blank on a bandsaw. I remove as much material and weight as possible and give it a circular shape. This could also be done with a chainsaw or on a lathe but it is much easier on the bandsaw and saves a lot of time and energy.

03 Next I mount the piece onto the lathe and make heavy cuts using a 16-mm bowl gouge to carve out the rough bowl shape. First, everything redundant is removed; then I refine the shape with lighter cuts using a 10-mm bowl gouge. This is a really exciting moment as it is the first glimpse I get of how well I located the bowl within the log.

04 A tenon is added to hold the bowl while the interior is hollowed out. Again, I start with heavy cuts to quickly remove material. I check the wall thickness by touch to ensure the bowl will dry equally and won't crack. The goal is to remove as much as possible but leave enough so the bowl can be made circular again after the wood has warped and changed to an oval shape during the drying process.

05 The bowl is now dried for several months in a controlled environment – somewhere cool

05

07

06

08

09

and draft-free. When I first started woodturning one out of five bowls cracked during the drying process; now it is about one out of a hundred. The bowl is then moved to a warm, well-ventilated place.

06 I use a nail chuck to mount the bowl back onto the lathe. First the warpage is removed. The next step is to establish the final shape. I switch to a freshly sharpened bowl gouge to achieve a good surface. The finer the surface the less sanding needs to be done.

07 I then do the same again but on the inside. I aspire to a consistent wall thickness that increases in the lower half by a few millimetres in order to ensure that the bowl will stand stably.

08 The next step is sanding. I start with 80 grit and sand up to 1500 grit depending on the wood and the future purpose of the bowl. This is often the least popular step of the process, but it needs to be done. I use power sanding to speed up the process, but it is still time-consuming.

09 Finally it comes to applying the finish. I have two different concepts when it comes to the finish depending on the purpose of the bowl. The first is a finish that ages well in daily use (good for salad bowls for example). I use a special blend of natural oils and waxes I developed myself. The second finish is one that helps the bowl keep its condition for as long as possible, but that doesn't age that well in daily use (best for gallery bowls for example). For this type I use modern hard wax oil developed for wooden floors.

FORGING A CAREER

My typical day starts with breakfast at 7 am. Before that, I do some yoga to maintain my physical condition (I want to still be able to turn wood when I am seventy). Then I go into my workshop. Tasks vary a lot throughout the year: during the springtime, for example, I process a lot of trees into bowl blanks. There are weeks of chainsaw work only and weeks where I am on the lathe to turn up to a hundred-and-sixty bowl blanks a day. I usually only stop to have lunch (when the whole family comes together), and finish work between 6 and 9 pm. Creativity may not always be at its best when you are working day in, day out. I therefore try to take a break from production for at least two or three weeks a year in order to try out new ideas and learn new techniques, which refreshes my mind and allows me to return with a new approach.

"There are lots of different ways you can supplement your revenue as a craftsperson"

My goal is to acquire most of my income from selling my work through my showroom and my online shop. People can order from my stock and I also accept bigger orders from companies. I don't do custom orders because I want people to buy my creations because they like what I do and not because I do what they like. That is quite a luxurious way of working if you are self-employed, so I also use other activities to make this attitude affordable. I work as a demonstrator for companies that sell woodturning machinery and occasionally do national and international seminars; I'm also self-employed as a maths tutor, mostly for pupils trying to pass their final exams; I work as an author, photographer, and as a professional photo model for fashion and lifestyle; last but not least, I do work as an influencer and content creator together with my girlfriend who is a professional photographer, graphic designer, and illustrator. There are lots of different ways you can supplement your revenue as a craftsperson.

I have also tried other methods for selling my work, such as small craft markets as well as large fairs. However in my experience there have only been a handful of profitable ones, which is the reason I tend to focus on my showroom and online shop. I ship pieces overseas every now and then but most of my pieces stay in Germany and the surrounding countries.

My income varies a lot throughout the year. In woodturning, Christmas business is up to eighty per cent of the annual income. This can be stressful since you have to spend and save money prudently. But I really enjoy the quieter time between Christmas and Easter, where I can produce with little interruption. If you are planning on becoming a professional craftsperson it is important to not do it for the money, because it is harder than you would imagine; passion and love are the only things that will keep you going.

SURVIVING IN THE MODERN WORLD

One of the most exciting things about woodturning is that you can combine modern technology with techniques that have been around for hundreds of years. I try to blend the best of the past and the present in my work; there are a lot of techniques and tools that have not changed much for centuries – the working principle of a lathe is not very different to a fire drill used in the Stone Age. A surface that has not been sanded but cut with a sharp tool on a lathe is way more durable and ages better when in frequent use. I really like the texture a sharp tool leaves on pole-lathe-turned objects and try to imitate it. But I would really miss the electric motor of my lathe – I find that it saves time and physical energy.

Everything is so fast-moving these days. For example, many of us feel the need to buy a new mobile phone every year as technology advances faster than ever before. As a result, people are looking for something more consistent and long-lasting. You might need a new computer every few years, but you can keep that wooden bowl for the rest of your life and maybe pass it down to your children. I think that craftsmanship helps people to ground themselves and slow down, which is why it will continue to be of interest. My customers don't belong to a specific demographic group or class – the only thing they have in common is an appreciation for the craft.

I am fortunate to have a large online following and be a published craftsperson with my own book. I never actively sought PR, but there seems to be something interesting about the fact that I am a young person in a traditional craft who looks a bit unconventional, and so there has always been a lot of interest from the media. Over the years I have had several hundred publications in print, online, and on TV. This is all very positive, but it is easy to mix up prominence with economic success. I don't think PR has ever had a huge influence on my business. In 2016 my first book was published, which had better effects on my business than all other publications in total, but not as much as you would possibly expect. In my opinion, the best way to spread the word about yourself is to be authentic and produce good-quality work all the time, to put a piece of your soul and your personality in everything you make, and to never give up.

CONSERVING THE CRAFT AND ITS LIVELIHOOD

In terms of community, there is a limited number of professional woodturning demonstrators; it is like a big family that meets several times a year, and whenever I go to do a demonstration I can be sure to meet a friend who is ready to help. People connect via internet forums and gather in big national and international meetings – there is a German woodturners meeting that takes place every two years and counts several thousand visitors. At the risk of sounding egoistic then, I don't worry too much about the importance of passing on my skill. There are so many hobbyist woodturners now that there is no need to be afraid that woodturning will die out in the near future. This does not mean that I don't want others to learn my craft and I also don't have a problem with giving away secrets. When I am asked questions I am always happy to help and share my knowledge. It's just I don't think that it is my task to do it actively. I never took up the craft for anyone else but myself.

In contrast, over-exploitation to natural resources, climate change, and invasive species are already big problems that potentially put craft under threat, and I hope there will still be wood to turn in twenty years' time.

CHAIR MAKING

One of the great things about handcrafted items is that they are often far more high quality and sturdy than mass-produced ones. Windsor chairs in particular are known to be long-lasting, with some originals that are hundreds of years old still in existence. Their durability comes from their structure. For most chair types, the rear legs and back support are of one piece, meaning all the stresses go into the joint that connects them to the rest of the chair. This is always the point at which most chairs will fail sooner or later. Uniquely, Windsor chairs have a solid timber seat into which the legs and back supports are inserted separately from each other as tenons into drilled mortises. This aspect, where all components are separate from each other yet joined sturdily at the seat, means there is no one weak spot being overworked.

"There is a sense of sending something useful into the future: an everyday object of comfort becoming beautiful in its familiarity, which will withstand the busy life of its owner and pass on to them a sense of satisfaction in their investment"

Bernard Chandley

BERNARD CHANDLEY

Melbourne, Australia | bernchandleyfurniture.com

Training: Apprenticeship in Carpentry/Joinery + Intensive courses with master craftspeople

Bernard Chandley is a maker of both traditional and contemporary Windsor chairs along with other fine furniture pieces, including Shaker-style benches and ornate cabinets. Striving to create pieces of heirloom quality, he was highly commended in the Clarence Prize for Excellence in Furniture 2017.

ORIGINS

I come from a large family of tradespeople. Between my parents, siblings, uncles, aunts, and cousins we cover a full gamut of usefulness. Fitter and turner, diesel mechanic, motor mechanic, boiler maker, plumber, electrician, carpenter, cabinet maker, bricklayer, panel beater, wool classer, fisherman, and lots of nurses. This made choosing to work in a trade an easy call. From a young age, I developed an affinity for making things from wood in my father's shed, from toys to toolboxes. At the age of sixteen, the idea of going bigger and getting paid for it was very appealing. I therefore left school to take up an apprenticeship in carpentry and joinery (with carpentry generally building onsite and joinery being focused more in a workshop).

Immediately it was the joinery component that made the biggest impression on me. Constructing house frames on site with my boss was rapidly moving away from the fastidious approach required for the pitching of a hardwood roof where strength and durability came through careful layout, cuts, and the interdependent nature of all the components creating the structure. Replacing such thoughtful work were pre-fabricated trusses and walls joined together by butt joints, nail guns, and metal fasteners. Such is the progress called for by economics. Meanwhile, back at trade school, in what seemed an archaic part of our training, we were taught to cut traditional joints by hand in order to understand their correct application, although having no place in which to apply them at that time. This concept of joining wood by utilizing its strengths and understanding its weaknesses resonated deeply and now, years later, is at the centre of my Windsor chair-making practice.

MOTIVATIONS

There is a simple logic to the structure of a Windsor chair; transfer the strength of the tree to the chair and you will have a strong chair. In all components of a Windsor chair you will find the grain running truly from one end to the other. Grain in a tree runs truly from top to bottom, which gives trees their strength and durability against the elements; if you cut along rather than across this grain when sourcing timber, the very fabric of the chair will be strong.

Combined with thoughtful geometry and well-fitted joinery, the resulting chair is light and flexible yet strong and durable. Durability means sustainability, and sustainability in furniture-making is rare in this age of disposable material objects. The opportunity to exert all my energy into designing and building deeply thought-through pieces utilizing proven, centuries-old techniques is incredibly satisfying. Having the belief that my efforts will lead to a chair outlasting myself drives me to be vigilant in my processes and thorough in their execution.

In making a chair for a client, there is a sense of sending something useful into the future: an everyday object of comfort becoming beautiful in its familiarity, which will withstand the busy life of its owner and pass on to them a sense of satisfaction in their investment. I cannot imagine working at something so arduous as Windsor chair making without being completely in love with the processes and methods of the making – the deep and varied knowledge required and the unique end product. No other chair functions in quite the same way.

With their solid timber seats in which all vertical components above and below terminate, you have a structure where all parts are separated from each other at the point at which a chair suffers most stress. Where they join horizontally it is at points to maximize bracing yet allow for flexibility. There is no other type of chair structure where the parts work together in isolation to make a strong and durable whole. Overcoming the complexity in the building of these chairs, finding ever-more efficient ways and means to complete them, is a never-ending and invigorating problem to solve. As with any form of woodworking, there is always a better or different way to reach the end. The fun is in discovery.

One of my favourite jobs is carving and shaping the seat. This is my opportunity to not only make it comfortable to sit on but also beautiful to gaze upon. The seat is the engine room of the Windsor chair. Everything begins and ends with it so to be able to shape it in such a way as to give it a sense of lightness while it does all the heavy lifting is endlessly fun. To some, a handmade Windsor chair may seem an unnecessary and overpriced indulgence in a world awash with affordable mass-produced furniture. But to me the chairs represent something important about us humans: our ability to think through problems and invent.

WORKSPACE AND TOOLS

Windsor-chair-making tools are designed perfectly and distinctly for their specific roles. The rough-out tools (that is, tools that remove the bulk of waste material before refining the actual shape) have open blades which follow the grain naturally, while those used for carving seats have curved blades necessary for hollowing. Open-bladed tools such as drawknives and scorps have a very intimate and honest relationship with the wood they are being worked with. Any deviation in the grain, defect, or change in density is made immediately obvious through the hands of the worker. With experience these tells become easy to interpret. They will also lead to a deeper understanding of the qualities of the wood, making the work both easier and more enjoyable.

The basic idea behind all woodwork is to firstly remove material quickly with coarse tools, even out and define the surfaces left behind with finer tools, and then refine to a finished state with finer tools yet. To successfully complete these tasks, holding devices are essential. In the case of spindles and arm and crest rails, the device used is a shaving horse, a centuries-old device familiar to quite a few greenwood crafts (see top-left image on right-hand page). It can come in a number of different configurations but the basic principal is that it is a foot-operated vice that allows quick release and grip from a seated position to aid in the shaping of a square section of wood into the round, in a quick and efficient manner. For seats, I move to my workbench, with its more conventional leg and tail vices and on which I am also able use F-clamps. At most times of the day you will find me working at either one.

01

03

02

04

PROCESS OVERVIEW

The importance of careful timber selection to the success of a Windsor chair cannot be overstated. However, finding the fast-grown, straight-grained timber required can be easier said than done. Whether purchasing green logs for splitting or large planks for milling, it is important to have good relationships with a number of different and varying timber merchants. When one doesn't have what you need, another might.

01 For traditional chairs, the process starts with open-bladed tools: metal wedges to split green logs, a froe to rive out component-sized pieces, and a drawknife to remove a lot of material quickly while sizing and roughly shaping parts of the chair such as spindles and arm and crest rails (see labelled illustration in the glossary for reference of chair components).

02 For contemporary chairs, I mark out parts on large kiln-dried boards from a timber yard. Kiln-dried timber is not as easily split as green wood though the need for continuous, straight grain remains. The job of breaking a board down therefore falls to machines. In the case of spindles, rails, and parts for turning, I use a bandsaw, which is really the most versatile machine in the workshop. Without the surety that comes with splitting and riving, great care must be taken in ensuring the grain is followed faithfully on the bandsaw.

03 To break down large stock into usable sizes, I either cut a log to rough lengths with a chainsaw before splitting it gradually into smaller sections for traditional chairs, or take a plank and break it down on the bandsaw for contemporary

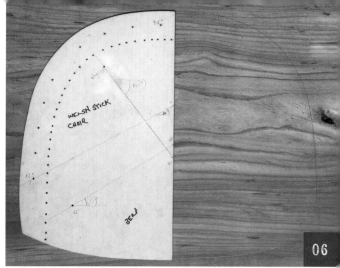

chairs, ready for work on the shaving horse or lathe.

04 I prepare parts that require steam-bending early in the process so that by the time the other work is done they are dried and set, ready for joinery and shaping. A wallpaper steamer provides continuous steam over the hour or more needed to soften the timber enough to bend it around a form made specifically for each different chair.

05 For traditional chairs, I turn the under-carriage, arm stumps, and posts on a lathe while the spindles are shaped by hand on the shaving horse. For my contemporary designs, I turn the spindles as well. Turning is an extremely efficient means of shaping wood in the round.

06 In preparation for joinery, I use templates for tracing the seat outline and marking out the position of the leg and spindle mortises. The templates for each chair contain all the information I need for drilling, including angles and sightlines for each mortise.

07 I then drill each mortise. There can be anywhere up to ten different angles on a Windsor chair. For example, the front legs are at a different angle to the rear legs; the spindles are at different angles depending on their position; and the posts and arm stumps all have their own angles as well. I use sightlines and a bevel and square to align myself correctly. Placing mirrors behind the bevel and square enables me to view them in line with the drill bit without needing to move my head. This allows for greater accuracy.

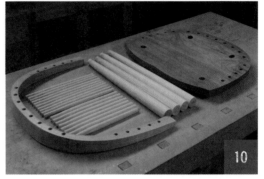

08 I then check how the legs fit in the mortises. The legs will run all the way through the seat where they are then wedged and trimmed off level with the seat top. The leg top (tenon), which runs through the seat, could be a cylinder shape fitted into a cylindrical hole that is drilled into the seat. However, by turning a six-degree taper into the leg top and then reaming a matching taper into the mortise, a sturdier join is made. This helps prevent any slippage which would see the leg top protrude through the seat top. Reaming is essentially widening or changing the shape of a hole. The reamer I use is a tapered tool with a cutting edge used for reaming a taper into the walls of a cylindrical hole.

09 For traditional chairs, the seat carving moves sequentially through an adze to break the surface and rough out the seat bowl, followed by the use of a scorp to continue the roughing out. For contemporary chairs, I cut the majority of material out with a rotary cutting blade mounted to a small angle grinder. In both cases, the carving is then refined with the use of a travisher, which with its housed blade protruding slightly through its curved sole rides over the roughed-out seat and reduces the high spots, bringing uniformity.

10 Once all parts are shaped and require only small refinements, and all the joinery has been test fitted, it is time to assemble the chair. I use liquid hide glue as it has a long open time, is reversible, and the set is long lasting. As there are numerous parts to a chair, assembly requires great concentration and a logical sequence. The final step, having cleaned, trimmed, and sanded everything following assembly, is to apply a finish. I generally want something that celebrates the beautiful natural product that wood is, that ages well, and that is easily repaired or replenished. I find a non-toxic oil/hard wax usually works well.

FORGING A CAREER

Were it not for an encounter with American chair maker and teacher Peter Galbert, I may never have come down this path of Windsor chair making. We met at a woodworking school in Melbourne where I was employed to make furniture and instruct. Back then, I was taking on furniture commissions of all shapes and sizes, though by the time I had participated in two of Peter's chair courses I had narrowed my focus to wishing to increase my knowledge on and build chairs. Even now, years later, I still view him as a mentor because his approach to his craft continues to inspire me. I believe that in any craft having a mentor can drive you forward more quickly than information from a book or video ever could. With their advanced skills and knowledge, a mentor can act as a point of destination. I feel it is always incumbent on me to improve, to understand more deeply, and to approach my work in a thoughtful manner.

My designs reflect a natural evolution in my knowledge and skills. While there have been points along the way where a combination of ambition and naiveté has found me scrambling to bring to fruition my own ideas, which in itself can be a great learning curve, efficiency in designing is as important as it is in making. Being patient and designing directly from my previous work, being able to rely more on my own experience and expertise, have cut down on research and development time dramatically. When designs are more ambitious I plan ahead carefully. Designing new chairs is at the pinnacle of satisfaction for me but I always bear in mind that I only get paid when I am actually building them for clients. Having a bread and butter product allows me to forge ahead with grander plans without the bottom falling out of the whole operation.

Building your clientele base is as fundamental as designing and building chairs. You can be the greatest maker in the world and starve to death without an audience. I once believed that without having my chairs in shop-fronts I would get nowhere. The problem with this concept is that the overheads that shopkeepers must pay can either lead to huge mark-ups on your own prices or, in order to keep the price reasonable, taking a hit from your own pocket while working just as hard but for less money. In any event I demurred and chose instead to rely on having a decent website and also the hit and miss of word of mouth. This was modestly effective as I built my client base, though it was not until I began utilizing social media that things began to truly take shape – for me, in the form of Instagram.

The incredible reach of this platform can't be overstated, and the format is perfectly suited to businesses needing exposure for their products but lacking the funds for PR campaigns or the desire to go down the aforementioned shop-front route. Even now, having used it for several years, I marvel at the ease with which I am able to present my work to not just a local but a global audience. The majority of my work now comes via people using hashtags as they search for the item they desire on Instagram. Besides the viability it has gifted my business, the other half of Instagram is the incredible international community it has created for craftspeople who otherwise work away in isolation. It has opened us all to new ideas, processes, and some truly phenomenal work we most likely would never have been exposed to otherwise.

SURVIVING IN THE MODERN WORLD

Furniture making can be practised in a staggering variety of ways using an equal variety of methods, so in order for it to become a sole source of income it is critically important to define for yourself exactly what it is you wish to make, why, and who for. An experienced furniture maker with several employees and the right setup can confidently take on a large array of jobs, but for a solo operator, having a range of pre-designed products makes far more sense. Finding ways to set yourself apart is worthwhile and could be through original design or by concentrating on work others may avoid. Happily for me, due to the difficulty of the work and the unique setup required, handcrafting chairs is not a job many furniture makers wish to tackle, and even less so for Windsor chairs.

Of course, the same reasons others avoid chair making have made pursuing it a challenge at times. But one I have relished. Speed and efficiency are hallmarks of any successful furniture business and handcrafted Windsor chairs don't automatically lend themselves to the former. I have had to find a balance between hand work and the use of machines, which is ever evolving. This began with a process of reducing the chairs down to their most essential and important qualities. Were I to teach someone to make a Windsor, I would always instruct them through the traditional techniques that have been handed down over centuries, as these will ensure a deep and lasting understanding of the material and the whys of the methods used to work it.

However, in making chairs full-time as a living it is important not to be dictated too much by nostalgia. You must be able to support yourself, and in some cases a family. I would never compromise the integrity of my chairs in order to get them finished more quickly, but where a job such as removing material can be done by machines more quickly and efficiently and in no way affect the outcome, I won't hesitate. Also, this is a very physical job that requires strength and dexterity, so using machines smartly can assist in the longevity of the business. Bodies do wear out! With the world population being what it is, mass-production goods make sense, but it makes no sense as a single-person workshop to aspire to the ways of mass production. It is impossible to compete on cost and output, so why try?

CONSERVING THE CRAFT AND ITS LIVELIHOOD

As someone who has been inspired to take up a craft by the example set by another, I am always conscious of the example I myself set. With most of my time taken up with making I use Instagram and Facebook to share a lot of my processes and am conscientious in depicting them in as comprehensible a way as possible. I try to create simple posts that I hope are instructive and interesting – then follow up by answering any questions I may receive. The advantage of this is two-fold: clients and prospective clients can watch as I build commissions and gain a deeper understanding of the work involved in completing their piece while building a sense of trust; and members of the maker community gain insights into my methods which may differ to their own.

Teaching is the most direct and thorough method for passing on the knowledge of the craft, though it is a discipline unto itself. The difference between building a chair alone in the workshop and teaching someone else how to build it is profound. Before attempting this, it is important to understand the ins and outs of what you do. It is important to have tested for yourself through first-hand experience, trial and error, the knowledge first passed on to you. An effective teacher should have deep comprehension of what they practice. With this in mind I began teaching prematurely in my opinion, stopped for several years, and am just now starting again. There is always more to know on any subject so keeping an open mind is important. In teaching a class I generally come away with more information than I went in with. It is always an exchange. The questions of students can act as a prompt to bring deeper clarity not only to them but to me also as I seek to explain the whys of a task.

LEATHER WORKING

Leather is a versatile material that has been used in a variety of forms over thousands of years, from creating bags, shoes, and saddles to being used in book-binding. Compared to many modern, synthetic materials it is highly durable. Variations between animal type and where the skin is taken from, in addition to natural deviations within a piece of leather, mean that each item created has its own personality.

"Every bit of leather is different; some is more flexible, or has a grain that goes in a certain way and won't do a certain thing. You come to learn how to read the material and use your knowledge to work out the best way to utilize it"

Lois Orford

LOIS ORFORD

Herefordshire, UK | benandloisorford.com

Training: Courses with Ben Orford & Mike Abbott + Self-taught

Lois crafts stunning leather sheaths and pouches for a variety of bushcraft activities, including knife holders, axe blade covers, and foraging bags. Working closely alongside her husband, Herefordshire knife maker Ben Orford (see page 42), she pulls functionality and style together by creating leather products that are designed to be as durable and hardy as possible. Her experience in green woodworking gives her an appreciation and admiration for the skill and creativity behind a multitude of crafts, and an understanding of what is most useful for those undertaking these tasks.

ORIGINS

I've always loved making things. One Christmas, when I was seven years old, I made a cabinet out of bits of wood and old nails; it was terrible! But the feeling of getting my hands on different materials and making something from them was irreplaceable. I like the outdoors, so I was a horticulturist and garden designer for twenty years before I returned to woodwork. Cold outdoor winters meant I was looking for something I could do inside more, so I attended a course run by legendary green woodworker Mike Abbott, and learned how to make chairs and tables. I then went on a leather-working course run by Ben Orford, and another course, and another course, working on various projects and discovering endless amounts of skill and enjoyment.

At the time Ben didn't enjoy making the sheaths for his tools as it took his time away from the metal and woodworking, so I took over this part. The cross-contamination of different materials made it difficult for Ben – metal workers' hands and clean leather don't go together. The beautiful thing about it is that you need one for the other: sharp blades require protective coverings and leather pouches are empty until you place something in them to make them functional.

MOTIVATIONS

Any craft where you start with something basic but end up with something functional and beautiful really excites me. Taking raw materials around you and creating something with your own hands and your own mind is a pleasure that is difficult to substitute. From a practical point of view, one of the best things about leather products is that they are much less bulky than chairs, and so easier to post out to customers and transport to shows.

Every bit of leather is different; some is more flexible, or has a grain that goes in a certain way and won't do a certain thing. You come to learn how to read the material and use your knowledge to work out the best way to utilize it. The sheaths I make are all the same but each one will be slightly different and will have been slightly different to make. This comes back to the individuality of leather working, and heritage crafts in general – the item you make is unique and the material you used to make it is unique.

Other craftspeople inspire me, as seeing what they do can change the way you are doing something, which improves your workflow. This means you are always evolving and there is a constant exchange of skills and ideas. Going to bushcraft shows means you are surrounded by talented people who have mastered working in a variety of materials. I will regularly see something someone else has made and think "Wow, I'd love to try that!" As an example, the medicine bags above were inspired by Native American pouches. I crafted them from antler and salmon skin sourced in the UK, bringing two stunning, natural materials together in harmony.

WORKSPACE AND TOOLS

I love my workshop – I'm fortunate to be able to have a large amount of my workspace in front of a window, which means I have lots of natural light and a beautiful view.

Above you can see my leather thinner, which allows me to reduce the thickness of a piece of leather (for example, from 4 mm to 2 mm), saving me having to buy lots of different pieces of leather in varying thicknesses. In order to cope with high demand I have invested in a couple of pieces of machinery to speed up parts of the process without taking away from the handmade element of my work. I used to cut every piece of leather out by hand, but I now have a press knife (bottom-right image on next page) cut to the shape I need, which means I can quickly cut the pieces of leather required by simply pushing down a lever (with some force required!). This also allows me to be more economical with the materials because you can get more out of each piece.

I also invested in a couple of sewing machines. However, I found that people prefer the look of the handmade ones. A main part of our brand is that the leather sheaths are meant to be as durable as possible, and the machine stitching wasn't as strong as the hand stitching. In this way you have to adapt and experiment with all the modern age brings.

Crafted With Passion for your next Adventure

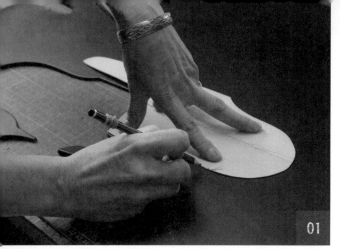

PROCESS OVERVIEW

01 To start I create a template, testing it as a piece of cardboard (usually an empty cereal box to be economical!) wrapped around the tool. Once I have the correct shape I draw round the template on the leather and cut it out with a knife or scissors. If I'm using a standard template I can simply use the press knife shown on the previous page to cut out the basic shape.

02 I then smooth off any rough edges on what will be the top edge of the sheath. I also press in a decorative line on top using a pair of dividers. I chamfer the edges with a bevelling tool. I also dye the top edge of the leather at this stage because I won't be able to do this once everything is stitched down.

03 I cut out another piece of leather called the welt. This is a strong piece of leather that will protect the stitches from the blade once the knife is inside. I glue this onto the side of the leather, fold it over, and clamp the sheath to leave it to dry. This is just to hold everything in place when I add the stitching.

04 I then smooth it on a grinder. I mark out the stitching with a pencil, using a double line in areas where extra strength is needed. The method I use is to punch all the stitching holes in one go using an awl. I find this easier and less labour intensive. Once I've gone all the way round I put it in a clam (like a clamp), which holds it in place while I do the stitching.

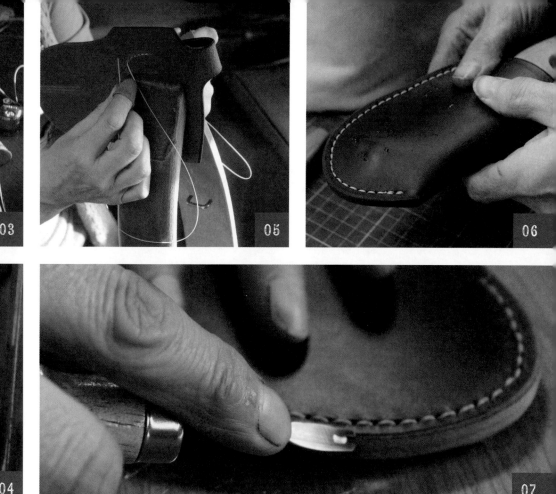

05 A traditional saddle stitch is best for the strength required for these kinds of sheaths. I use one length of thread with a needle on each end, with one needle through one side and the other needle on the other side but passing the thread over. This creates a sort of overhand knot within the leather, making the stitching super strong as it won't easily unravel. I then use an edge beveller to chamfer the edges all around.

06 With the knife wrapped up in cellophane to protect it, I dip the sheath in a bowl of hand-hot water. I use leather that is tanned with vegetable matter, which means it goes floppy in water. It also means it has fewer chemicals on it as I like to work with materials that are more organic.

I mould the leather around the knife – not too tightly, creating smooth transitions. I also add our logo while it's wet – it's always important to add your mark on what you have made. I then remove the knife and dry the sheath behind a wood-burning stove, somewhere constantly warm. Once dried, the leather will hold its shape; it's a similar process of heating and cooling to manipulate the materials' molecules that we use in the knife-making process (see pages 48–49).

07 Finally I add the finishing touches, dyeing the edge again and buffing it off with a burnisher. I apply leather balm to re-nourish the dried-out leather, polish it up, and once I'm happy with it the sheath is ready to be sent out to a customer.

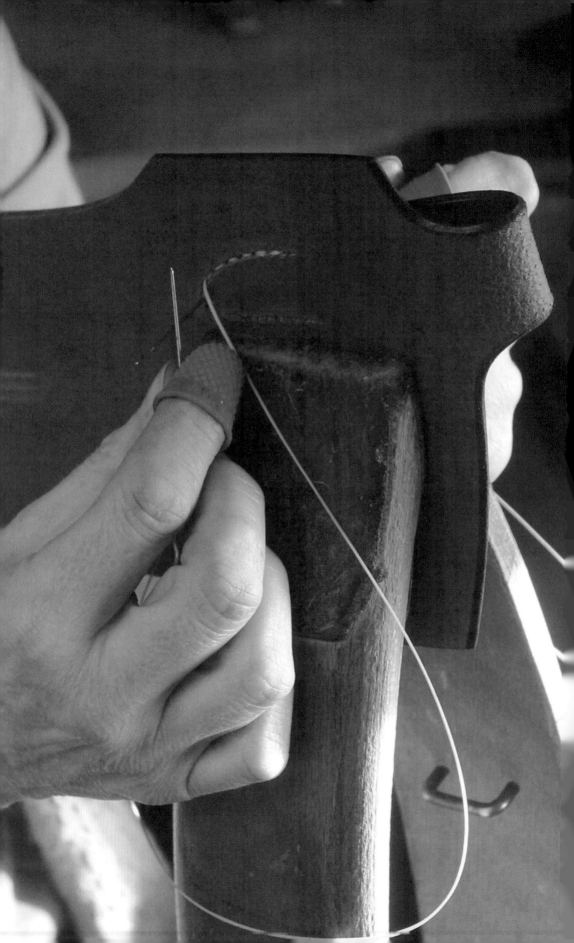

FORGING A CAREER

Our tool-making and leather-working combination became a living organically – people saw our products at shows and liked them. When we first started out it was difficult, with lots of hard work for little gain. We would travel two hundred miles and would consider selling a couple of knives a big achievement. It is important to persevere though. At each show we went to we sold a little bit more, which encouraged us.

Start practising the craft as a hobby and let it evolve naturally; gradually begin to make money from it and grow your craft over time until you can live from it. There are ways you can help develop an income and reputation other than direct selling, such as through running courses, attending relevant shows, and writing articles for magazines. It is important to think about your vision rather than comparing it to that of others all the time. It is all about individuality and your creativity. If you want to get an apprenticeship, keep asking people – pursue your passion as much as you can; work for free if you need to and are able to.

Self-employment doesn't work for everyone but I have always enjoyed the mix of home and work. You have got to be absolutely in love with what you are doing. Even when we are away we get inspired and talk about what we are going to make when we get back. It is part of who we are. The only time I really experience stress is in the run up to a show. This is largely because of the great expectations we put on ourselves – we always want to give people as much as we can through demonstrations and want to ensure we don't disappoint people if they were looking to buy a specific item. It is very rewarding when we see how enthusiastic customers and attendees are though.

"It's okay to make mistakes as long as you don't keep making the same ones again and again"

One of the hardest things about being a craftsperson is that you aren't just making things; you have got to keep a website up to date, respond to high numbers of emails, deal with paperwork and tax, and a whole world of other responsibilities. It is worth noting as well that due to the nature of traditional crafting, you have to be mentally strong when something goes wrong after six hours' work and you have nearly finished your piece; there's no way back if you do it wrong unfortunately. At the same time, remember that it's okay to make mistakes as long as you don't keep making the same ones again and again.

SURVIVING IN THE MODERN WORLD

Social media has had a massive influence on our livelihood. It makes it much easier to get your name and brand out there. We often feel like we are in our own little world when we are in our workshop, but now when we go to shows lots of people have discovered us and engaged with us online so they already know who we are and what we are about. It's like meeting up with friends you've just not met in person before, and the support and excitement from them is very warming.

We like to help people out so we always encourage people to ring or email us if they become stuck on something so we can help them if we can. This makes us stand apart from a huge, faceless online retailer. We also put a lot of thought into the way our products are packaged and gift-wrapped, and like to include a handwritten message with each one because we are genuinely grateful that someone is buying from us. This touch of individuality is something we find people crave, especially in a world where a lot of things are automated and lack personality.

One element to consider in the twenty-first century is the sustainability of materials. I have been sampling new leathers to move over to ones that are more ethically sourced, with a higher care of the animals it comes from. The quality of leather from British, outdoor-bred animals is astonishing. It means they have been out in all weathers so the graining and fibres make it unbelievably strong. It is good to know the farmers you source from and make sure you are aware of and satisfied with the chain of custody of your materials. That said, with our growing range of customer requests, sometimes you can't use leather and you need to use composites instead – for example in the jungle leather will just rot. It is interesting to use a mixture of modern and traditional materials, and master the skills associated with each of these.

CONSERVING THE CRAFT AND ITS LIVELIHOOD

Preserving and cultivating our heritage and crafts is important today because it quenches an increasing desire for escapism in modern society. More and more people are getting into crafts and doing things with their hands. I think this is because we spend all our time chasing things to tick off – getting a mortgage, paying bills, making a pension plan: you've got everything you should have, but there's just something missing. Craft nourishes something that none of that other stuff can fulfil. There is something ancient in our minds that wants us to create; making things is innate, and when you don't feed that you can find that you have everything but at the same time don't have anything. Many crafts you can just do in your living room, such as basket weaving, which makes them very accessible to people who want to give heritage crafts a try.

Many artisans refuse to take on apprentices because they believe it can take away from your market. However, I don't believe apprentices will steal our business; other people using our techniques and ideas just makes the market bigger because more people get to see the knives and their leather sheaths, and so it broadens our audience.

RUTH PULLAN

Yorkshire, UK | www.ruthpullan.co.uk

Training: Cumbria School of Saddlery with Master Saddler David May + Other
heritage craft courses

Ruth Pullan launched her stylish brand in 2012 and creates hand-stitched, natural leather goods made with British materials. Learning from craftspeople who work in ceramics, glass, textiles, basketry, wool craft, green wood, precious metals, and iron has influenced how she works and views her craft in historical and contemporary contexts. In 2018 Ruth converted a van into a leather workshop, allowing her to travel the country sharing her products and expertise.

ORIGINS

Throughout my childhood and teenage years, I had always been interested in art and design and enjoyed making things, but did not really have any idea of where that could lead in adulthood. On leaving college I got a job at a gallery which sold handmade jewellery from independent craftspeople around the UK and Europe. It was so eye opening and inspirational to see these craftspeople making a living from what they loved doing. The job allowed me the time and the funds to go on all sorts of craft courses, from green woodworking to blacksmithing, and I met some great people along the way who encouraged me in what I was doing. On reflection, it was my own way of doing a degree and a very influential time.

As my knowledge and interest in heritage crafts started to grow, I went to the Cumbria School of Saddlery to learn how to work with leather in a traditional way so that I could create handles for the tweed bags I had started making; I never looked back. Leather work is the perfect mix of minimal tools and processes: no machines, a beautiful material that only gets better with age, and resulting products that can last a lifetime – a good antidote to the throwaway fashion I was becoming ever more aware of at the time.

MOTIVATIONS

There are many aspects of my work that I enjoy, not least the fact that with minimal tools and space I can create products which can last a lifetime. Leather is a primal material and one which as humans we have worked with for a long time. It is the perfect material for making hard-wearing and long-lasting items while having a character and aging with the user as they are handled, something which plastic alternatives can't come close to matching. Leather work allows your creative instinct to shine within a framework of methods and skills that you need to hone and practise until they become second nature. There is nothing better than the quiet and meditative process of methodically stitching away in my workshop; hours can go by without me noticing.

"I think that handmade objects can and do tell stories of the past and are very important because of that"

It is not just the making and the process which keeps me going though; it is the bigger picture of how my work can fit into a wider network of makers and craftspeople who are reviving some of the old ways of life in contemporary surroundings. When I was first learning leather work I read books by Dorothy Hartley, who went around the British Isles documenting rural crafts in the thirties. I was inspired by the rural and town communities of craftspeople who used local materials to make the things they needed and how these crafts all interlinked in the local economy. It is easy to be nostalgic for a time I have not even lived through. However, I think there is a lot to be learnt from how these resilient and local economies worked and I love being a part of that revival in my own way.

It can of course be easy to over intellectualize an essentially very practical activity, and it happens too often perhaps, but I think that handmade objects can and do tell stories of the past and are very important because of that. All of this history is in each of us. It is because we were able to make things that we have become who we are. We all still carry with us a need to create and use our hands and I feel very privileged to be able to tap into that ancestral heritage and energy through making.

WORKSPACE AND TOOLS

I converted a van into a mobile leather workshop in 2018 and in doing so achieved a long-held ambition to create a mobile space from which I can make and teach. It feels like it is the culmination of years of learning different crafts and the people I have met. There are beautiful objects around me – pots, spoons, bowls, and plates – all made by woodworking friends of mine. And my view can be anything I want it to be.

Being able to work from such a small space highlights the few tools I need. My main tools include my saddler's knife, which I use to cut the leather. Its design allows intricate shapes to be cut – as long as it is kept sharp! My awl is very special to me. I use it to make holes for the stitches. The handle was turned by the carpenter who had his workshop next to the saddler I learnt from. The pricking iron I use to mark the rows of stitches was made to a traditional English pattern and helps to create uniform rows of stitches. These three tools, along with some needles, a hide mallet, a cork block (I use this to provide support behind the piece I am working on when I am making the holes, so that the awl can go through cleanly and is not blunted on the work mat), a little tool to bevel edges, and a cutting mat are almost all I use. It is important to me to only use tools which, if I had to, I could attempt to make myself. I think using a small array of tools encourages me to use them skilfully and imaginatively for different applications.

PROCESS OVERVIEW

01 The leather I buy comes in shoulders of around fifteen square feet. Not all of this is usable though and I have to select the most suitable areas for the item I am making. For this purse I want something that will not stretch too much with wear. I also look for interesting features in the leather that I know will weather nicely over time. Once the area has been selected I mark the pattern using a scratch awl.

02 I then cut out the pieces using a saddler's knife. It is a great tool that is brilliant at cutting intricate shapes as well as long straight cuts. The tool is used in a rocking motion and is a joy to use.

03 The leather comes to me as "tooling shoulder", meaning that it has not been dyed or conditioned. It is up to me to work different oils, fats, and

beeswax into it to give it a water-resistant finish that weathers beautifully over time. I used to dye leather but have come to love the undyed material as it is and how it develops a patina over time.

04 The edges of the leather need to be bevelled and burnished to avoid becoming scuffed, to prevent water marks, and also because aesthetically it is very pleasing to see a polished, smooth edge. It is tactile and makes a significant difference to how the end product feels in the hand.

05 Before gluing and stitching the piece together, I glue and stitch on any hardware I want to include. Whether it is buckles, loops, or studs, they are all made from sand-cast brass at Abbey Foundry in Walsall, one of the last remaining buckle foundries in the UK.

06 The stitches are marked on the pieces using a pricking iron before they are assembled and glued using pearl glue – a natural product made from rendered sinew, bones, and hide trimmings. I have gradually stopped using oil-based products such as dyes and contact adhesives in my work, preferring to use only natural products and especially those derived from the cow itself. The cow provides us with these products, which are perfect for the purpose, so why use artificial substances as a substitute? I also believe that if an animal is to be killed then we should use every last part of that animal.

07 I make the holes for the stitches using a diamond-shaped awl; this is the key to making the stitching very neat. I was taught the traditional technique of holding the work in clamps and making each hole and stitch individually while holding the awl and needles together. I found it hard to get the stitching consistent however, so I developed my own method of making all the holes in one go.

08 For the stitching, I use the traditional English saddlery stitch, which involves using a long piece of thread, threaded with a needle at either end.

09 Once everything is stitched, the edges get a final burnish and the whole item is polished with a cloth. It is then ready to be sent to the customer. Packaging is very important to me – it is the first impression people get of something when they receive it in the post. I always write a little note to the customer to personalize it.

FORGING A CAREER

I started off by attending a lot of fairs, meeting the public and getting feedback on my products. I also had a number of stockists and made all sorts of commissions for people. That really broadened my skills. This was all necessary when starting out but it was very exhausting! I now have a few stockists who really know me and my work, produce a small collection that I sell online, and do very few fairs or exhibitions; but I make a good living for myself and enjoy it a lot more. Sometimes feeling busy doesn't mean you are successful. A simpler business model can be more effective and leave time for other things that keep you fresh and excited about your work.

I have learnt to be flexible and take opportunities when they come along. I have a little checklist of why I am doing what I am doing and I find this really useful, especially when I am making a decision about what my next step would be – I can just go through the list and see if the opportunity ticks the boxes. It is really easy to lose sight of motivation, and the enjoyment can wane because of it. I think it is important to tell your customers what your ideals are too. More often than not you will get loyal customers, who believe in you and your product, coming back to buy more for friends and family as a result. It is the best compliment a maker can get.

"If you have the skills, modest expectations for your business and life, produce a good product and enjoy what you do, then there is no reason why you should not succeed"

One thing that is very important for me is to have variety in my work. I teach regularly, which is a great balance to the more solitary work in the workshop, and I also organize a countryside crafts and skills festival in the Yorkshire Dales. These aspects provide support to my leather work and allow me to make the things I want to make and have the life I want to lead. This way, it is sustainable for me and I know leather work will always be a part of my life.

If you have the skills, modest expectations for your business and life, produce a good product and enjoy what you do, then there is no reason why you should not succeed.

SURVIVING IN THE MODERN WORLD

Technology has brought many great things that you can utilize to good effect as a craftsperson. Online banking and payments make transactions quick and simple and social media means that we can get to our customers easily and cheaply compared to expensive advertising. I would not have been able to make the decision to have a mobile workshop if I could not have access to mobile broadband and my online shop. It means I can be anywhere and sell my work. I don't have to have a commitment to rent for a fixed-term contract and the overheads are comparatively less.

However, although my virtual shop allows me to have a physical shop every day, it cannot compete with face-to-face contact, particularly when selling handmade, tactile objects. People need to feel the product, smell it, and try it on for size. It is really important to have opportunities for the maker to meet the customer and your customer to meet you too; so much more can be said face to face than over the internet. It is this aspect of customer relations that can make you stand out from any other product that can only be bought online.

In terms of the physical process of making, I am less enticed by technology. Sometimes I wonder about having the patterns cut from the hides using laser machines and then me coming in to assemble them by hand. For me, however, I think this would have a huge impact on how I feel about the end product. I would not have the same knowledge of the piece of leather; I would not have been able to select the best parts of the hide. There are some things a computer just can't do, especially when it comes to such a wonderfully variable material as leather.

Sometimes being a maker can be difficult in that you are a company where there is just one person designing, researching, making, marketing, designing and building a website, and selling. Eventually, I would like to be part of a cooperative of makers and growers who pool their resources and skills together to provide for a local market, limiting waste, packaging, and transport burdens and reducing the workload for each individual business.

CONSERVING THE CRAFT AND ITS LIVELIHOOD

I think teaching and passing on skills to others is a big part of conserving crafts, not just for the obvious reason of other people then knowing the skills themselves, but also because we live in an age where people have forgotten that we used to make so much ourselves and be so much more self-sufficient. On many of my courses I have found that the act of learning a bit about a craft makes people have a new-found respect for those who do it as a living, and also makes them think differently about buying cheap, mass-produced items. I think this is so important. A large part of my workshops involves explaining where leather comes from and the ethical and ecological implications of choosing products that have been made using mass-produced leather from environmentally toxic processes. Teaching craft skills means people have an understanding of how to repair things too, meaning less waste and less financial burden from having to replace things.

I have really enjoyed teaching people over the last few years, from groups of bushcraft enthusiasts in a woodland workshop to young children at a festival. It is great in particular to teach those who at school were told that they were not any good at art or making things but then produce a beautifully stitched and finished item. The look of immense satisfaction that they have on their face, having made something that they will use every day, using their own hands, is priceless. I love the afternoons on my workshops where everyone is happily stitching away, perhaps with a cup of tea and putting the world to rights. It is what we have done for millennia. Craft and the need to create the world around us to our own design are what make us human.

CORACLE MAKING

A coracle is, by definition, a small keel-less craft propelled by one person using a single paddle. Traditionally the light framework would have been constructed of bent sticks (hazel, ash, and willow) and a cover of animal hide. Modern materials such as fibreglass are often used today to produce a very light craft with little or no maintenance. Some eighteen different designs have been identified throughout the British Isles and evolved to suit the local river they sail upon; allied craft are found throughout the world. It is quite feasible that these fascinating vessels, in some form or other, were bobbing about thirty thousand years ago. The stronghold of British coracles is in West Wales, where they are still worked in tandem using nets to catch salmon and sea trout.

"Out of water a coracle is more curiosity than boat, like a beached whale; put it on water and it comes to life in skilful hands... Once in a coracle, the stress and strain of our modern lifestyle simply melt away"

Peter Faulkner

PETER FAULKNER

Herefordshire, UK

Training: Interviews with Eustace Rogers + Self-taught

Master coracle maker Peter Faulkner initially began a career working on a deep-sea oil tanker fleet in the Merchant Navy before moving into insurance and later becoming a teacher. It was only in his forties that Peter made his first coracle in which he travelled eighty-five miles down the river Teme – just for fun. Besides his obvious skill and astounding attention to detail, Peter's charismatic personality and sense of humour make him a remarkable individual to meet; it is clear why he has found himself featured in publications and TV shows such as *Country Living* magazine, James May's *Man Lab*, and *Wild River* with Ray Mears to name but a few. After taking a short break from his craft business, Peter has eagerly taken up the paddle again to continue his journey.

ORIGINS

My path towards coracle making can definitely be traced back to my childhood. My parents owned a local shop in the village, and as soon as we had finished our chores my brothers and I would be out of the house, into the countryside. I spent a lot of time by the river in the summer and hours and hours in the woods. We ran wild and had no fear, only coming home at mealtimes – it was a huge freedom and where I acquired my interest in the natural world.

On moving back to the village in 1985, the desire to make the most of nature returned. I had seen a TV programme on great river journeys and decided I wanted to travel down a local river myself. I wasn't sure what to travel in. I considered a raft, but then in 1987 I traced a coracle maker, Eustace Rogers, living in the Ironbridge Gorge on the River Severn. Eustace took me to his workshop and eagerly showed me his traditional Ironbridge coracles constructed of ash laths and covered with calico sealed with bitumastic paint. I wasn't overly enthusiastic; but then came the Damascus moment: suddenly I saw, leaning against a wall, a hide-covered coracle. That was it – my voyage would be done in such a vessel. Over three visits to Eustace I filled a small notebook with notes, line drawings, and measurements. With all this information and sound advice, I eventually completed a very rustic but totally waterworthy coracle. I still have that notebook, a prized possession indeed.

Once I had made my own coracle, I travelled down the river Teme, raising money for charity. I enjoyed it so much that I then tried the Severn, the Wye, the Thames, and the Spey. There was much camaraderie and friendship when doing these trips. Each river is like a long village and news travels very fast up and down the waterway by way of the "bush telegraph". It is unusual to do such journeys in such a tiny boat but, besides appeasing my wanderlust, it proves the craft's waterworthiness.

MOTIVATIONS

When I first saw a raw-hide coracle leaning up against the wall of Eustace's workshop, it was love at first sight. I have always liked water, so the idea of a boat appeals naturally to me anyway. Out of water a coracle is more curiosity than boat, like a beached whale; put it on water and it comes to life in skilful hands. It is not, however, designed for speed. Speed usually means noise. Once in a coracle, the stress and strain of our modern lifestyle simply melt away and, as my very first customer – John Leach the potter – said, you see the river from the inside.

I love working with natural materials, and the boat fits perfectly into that niche because there are so many different skills involved – selecting hazel from deciduous woodland; handling and shaping natural, sustainable wood; cleaning and plaiting horse hair; choosing, preparing, and curing raw hide. Natural materials are constantly teaching and testing you; it is never a case of you teaching them. I have always been impetuous with a job, eager to get started and stuck in. Harvesting materials, prepping them, and finally fitting them together to create a waterworthy craft have taught me patience and humility. This is the nature of coracle making: you can't jump; every stage has to be done in strict order.

"My business motto is *liberatus et pulcritudo* – freedom and beauty, which is essentially what a coracle represents"

The range of materials also means there are distinct personalities among different coracles – different horse hair and different hides allow each one to be unique; similarly, the grain of the ash used for the seat is like a fingerprint and means that there are never two seats the same. There is also a print of the maker in each creation. I have made around three hundred coracles over the years and each one has its number burnt into the seat or pillar in Roman numerals. They are all registered in a notebook chronologically with the customer's details; I have never had a computer.

When you have a nice hide alongside all the natural colours of the wood, a coracle is a very beautiful thing to look at; but it is also a practical boat. My business motto is *liberatus et pulcritudo* – freedom and beauty, which is essentially what a coracle represents. My logo is a swallow in flight, also reflecting these components. I would not ever want to be in the business of just churning out boats – I like to balance the making with other interesting activities like paddling down rivers. Voyages so far total six hundred miles.

I also enjoy the challenge coracles present. I consider myself a very practical person, with a reasonable brain for solving problems. I initially just copied what I had seen, but then I found better and easier ways of doing things and ways to make the coracle stronger. I am a perfectionist – if I can't do something properly to the best of my ability, I would rather not do it.

WORKSPACE AND TOOLS

My workshop for the past fourteen years has been the old village school room – the very school I attended as a child of six. With kites and buzzards wheeling overhead you can sometimes hear the distinctive call of peregrine falcons playing high above. Other workspaces have included my mother-in-law's back garden, a Victorian granary, and a converted stable block. My wife, Vivienne, and I also own a wildflower meadow where I have my own willow bed to harvest from, by the side of which flows a clear prill (a small stream) that never runs dry; it flows into the Teme half a mile away.

I have never craved after expensive, sophisticated tools. Most of mine are bought at flea markets – they soon become old friends when used regularly. The most valuable and used tools are of course my own hands. Apart from that, my first and favourite tool is a small hand axe that I bought in a bric-a-brac shop in Swanage. The old steel gives an edge like a razor and its main use is in the process of paddle making. I also harvested all my coppiced hazel with it for many years until I bought some more modern loppers. Several specialist tools are needed in each process of construction, including sacking needles, fleshing knives, a drawknife, sharpening steel, hollow fids, and a sailor's sewing palm. Over the past thirty years I have gathered an interesting selection. I keep my hoard to a minimum however so that each tool has a specific job to make the task in hand as simple as possible. I aim for minimum effort and complexity to achieve the best result. I also have a fondness for interesting and unusual tins to store small tools and materials in.

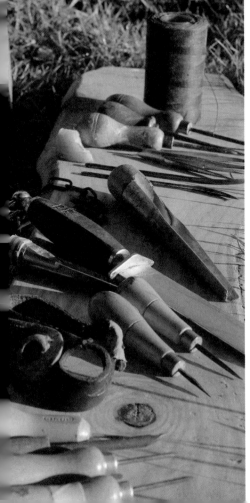

PROCESS OVERVIEW

01 Harvesting and preparing materials comes first. March is a good time to cut hazel wands, which will form the main frame of the coracle. I keep the wands outside for up to three months to season out; then they will bend beautifully. When fresh the bark is too soft and is easy to damage, plus the sugar from the sap is a rotting agent.

02 I harvest willow legs for the gunwale (the boat's rim) and boat floor annually from my own willow bed. The willow has to be graded for different thicknesses so it will work consistently into the boat framework. Seven meters of plaited horse hair will also be needed to lash the hide onto the framework. I source and prepare the hair myself. It is amazingly strong and waterproof, while still offering elasticity.

03 I obtain hides from the village butcher, Douglas. Each hide has to be measured and meticulously checked for holes. The hide is then power-hosed to remove dirt. At this stage the hide is heavy and difficult to handle, so it is hung over a bar to drain until it feels like a damp chamois. The critical process of "fleshing" then takes place, where the hide is draped over a table and all the surplus fat is scraped off using a butcher's knife. It then goes into a salt bath for five days.

04 To construct the frame, I bend hazel up from a template on the table I work on. If the hazel has become very dry, I use a hot-air blower to warm it up gently so it bends as if it is fresh. The curvature has to be almost perfect all the way round for the boat to be functional and balanced.

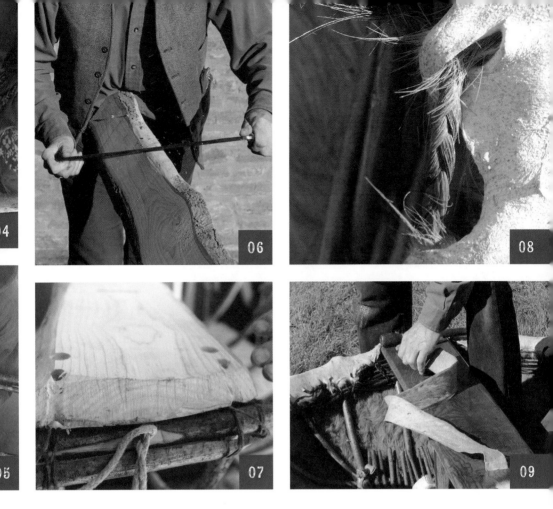

05 Once the hazels are tied the rim goes on and is firmly secured in place by pillars and cords. Each wand is then lashed to the rim until all the ends are firmly in place. The willow rim is then woven in using forty-eight rods.

06 I cut the ash seat out of a plank using a bandsaw, and use an axe, drawknife, and spoke shave to finish it off. The ash paddles are fashioned using the same hand tools. The priest, crafted with similar tools, is a simple yew club used for dispatching fish when caught; you don't want a 20 lb salmon thrashing about in a small coracle.

07 The ash seat is then lashed onto the framework. At last the coracle framework is removed from the worktable and the willow floor

is woven in, followed by some final trimming and adjustment.

08 I take the hide out of the salt bath and wash the salt out. It then goes on a drying pole. I place the whole hide over the coracle framework and lash it on. The excess hide is trimmed off and put aside until later for the straps. Holes are then punched all the way round the hide using a chisel. The seven-metre plaited horse-hair cord is then laced through the hide and around the frame. I mould the hide on rather than stretching it to avoid distortion of the frame.

09 Finally, the hide straps are cut to shape. You have to allow for shrinkage when attaching them using hazel pegs.

FORGING A CAREER

When I made my first coracle I had not even thought of making a second one. It was just a one off to achieve my ambition and help me get down a river. The orders just trickled in. As jobs continued to come in I decided to make a business out of it alongside my full-time teaching job, making coracles mainly at the weekends and in the evenings during the summer. It is surprising what you can do when you want to. When I retired as a teacher I was working long days for six days a week in the summer; it was very physically intense, even though it was seasonal.

All coracles are generally made to order. I sometimes receive commissions from places like heritage museums. I began making currachs (a sea-going boat made with the same materials as a coracle) in 1996 and consequently received invitations to maritime festivals. This was a good opportunity to build up the business and opened up a whole new world for me and my wife – we went to boat festivals and shows in Norway, Germany, Finland, and France. I also ran a course in Slovakia. We met new people and made new friends.

As word got out, I found myself being approached by production companies for films and TV shows. I made coracles for the film *Snow White and the Huntsman* and *Treasure Island* with Eddie Izzard, and was able to make a coracle with James May to cross the Taymar in Plymouth. I love doing that sort of work and it acts as a good shop window. However, I have to make sure I cover my expenses, and work out mileage and accommodation. I'm a rarity, and sound knowledge and experience must be acknowledged and awarded accordingly.

"There must be a certain mystery and allure about coracles that draw people to them and their makers"

In addition to my usual commissions, customers want to make their own under my instruction, which is why I run courses. Enthusiasts have come from the US and New Zealand to make their own coracle. There must be a certain mystery and allure about coracles that draw people to them and their makers. Someone from Scotland came down just to meet me in person. Another person was writing a historical novel set in the Stone Age and wanted first-hand experience of making one so they could include it in their book.

If I had to actually go out and buy my materials it would be very expensive. The willow bed is my own and I usually give the hazel landowners a suitable gift for their permission to harvest that. I try to find ash logs that have already fallen. The hides are not too expensive and horse hair is cheap. There are still outgoings that need to be monitored though, such as workshop rent, accountancy fees, and keeping the van on the road. I also need to make sure I cover my time – it takes a total of around fifty hours to make a coracle, including harvesting and preparing the materials.

SURVIVING IN THE MODERN WORLD

I am fortunate enough to have an outgoing personality, which helps when working with the media and meeting the general public. I have over thirty years of experience teaching in the special needs sector, along with experience in amateur dramatics and the world of folk music and dancing. Helping out in our family shop as a youngster meant that I talked to, and found things in common with, a whole range of different people from varying backgrounds. This exposure to a public presence has helped me to easily adapt to more public-facing projects.

"I always like to improve methods where I can but the outcome has to be simpler"

In contrast to the increased pace of modern-day life, with craft you have to have control over the amount you produce, otherwise there is no pleasure. Every little bit of wood has its own character so you have to work your way into the material and find out how to manipulate it, staying alert all the time. You don't want to snap things or get anything wrong – it is important to learn from your mistakes as it is painstaking to fix them. I am always being tested and that is what makes it interesting and challenging. I always like to improve methods where I can but the outcome has to be simpler. I'm a bit of a purist and believe in simplicity; too much technology kills the germ of creativity.

Coracle making is a very physical undertaking. Long-distance running has helped to maintain my fitness over the years, as has coracle sailing itself. An expert in a coracle makes its propulsion seem effortless; do not be deceived. The muscles from the heels to the nape of the neck are all in play. Considering the physical toll of a craft and how you can sustain yourself at a certain level is important.

CONSERVING THE CRAFT AND ITS LIVELIHOOD

Being part of a community of makers has a lot of benefits to an individual craftsperson. I am part of a network of coracle makers and we all help each other out, referring customers to the appropriate creator. There is also a shared enthusiasm for things that are handmade that is warming and enlightening.

The appreciation of coracles and other crafted items has certainly been on the rise, and is a slow-growing trade as it comes into the public eye more with TV and media coverage. With coracles, people seem to be interested in something created from hide and natural materials. I don't think this interest will die off; it will just reach a certain level. Some people just aren't interested, however.

I would like to take on an apprentice to teach them everything I know, but they would have to be vetted first. There are various grants available to make this viable for people who want to learn. When Eustace Rogers died there was nothing left after his family had spent generations making coracles, which highlights the importance of passing on the knowledge. I bless the day back in February 1987 when I walked down his garden path for the first time to meet him.

BASKET MAKING

In almost every civilization throughout history, woven baskets have been used for work, leisure, and domestically at home. The materials grown to make them, including the most popular, willow, tend to be perishable so there is no way to tell exactly the true age of this intricate, versatile craft. As no two pieces of natural material are the same, every basket is truly unique and always will be, which is what makes them one of a kind and special to their owner. For the same reason a basket weaver can take never ending satisfaction from the vast array of variations in their creations.

"The history of basket making is something that is important to me – it is a real, honest, and local craft, representing knowledge, tradition, and pride"

May Tove Lindås

MAY TOVE LINDÅS

Søgne, Norway | skudeneset-gaard.no

Training: Course with Steen Madsen Dk through Tradisjonshåndverk

---

Expert weaver May Tove Lindås created her first basket just as a way to progress onto making items for her initial love, gardening. However, May was captivated, and today runs her own basket-making business from a beautifully renovated nineteenth-century barn. In addition to weaving the baskets, May continues the work of her Norwegian ancestors by growing and harvesting her own willow, and teaching the technique of weaving to others.

ORIGINS

As a child I experienced great pleasure in being outdoors, and spent a lot of time in the woods and mountains. My father was very knowledgeable, and willingly taught me about the surrounding nature. An interest in gardening and floristry came early, and later this became my profession. By coincidence I came across the trade of basket making. It all started when I received the book *Living Willow Sculpture* by Jon Warnes as a gift. I loved this book, which showed how trees could be shaped into fascinating sculptures. Many pieces made out of willow began to appear in my garden.

Willow is a beautiful material that can be easily processed and shaped. You can very quickly make fascinating installations that fit naturally in gardens and outdoor spaces. A gift for the impatient gardener who seeks a quick and finalized result, the characteristics of willow make it ideal for outdoor settings where aesthetic values combine with functionality.

In my first willow-weaving class I had no intention of weaving a basket. I wanted to learn techniques that could be useful for my gardening work. Luckily, I was told by the trainer that I first had to weave a basket, and then I could work with garden installations. And that was how my first basket was made, unintentionally. I was hooked, completely overwhelmed by the characteristics of this fabulous species of tree – a wood that can be processed and made so flexible that you can make a knot with it.

MOTIVATIONS

I have always been creative. Making something with your own hands is a passion for me. One of the things I love about basket making is that you can create just about any shape you like, everything from natural, organic shapes to abstract and square ones. You can experiment with different materials and textures, and combine basket making with other crafts. The harvesting of willow is hard work. But when you have a whole storage room filled with bundles of willow, in ten different variations, it makes it all worthwhile. The many thousands of stalks that in a year's time are going to be transformed into beautiful baskets of many shapes and colours are a truly rewarding sight.

In the workshop no two days are alike. Some are filled with course participants eager to learn; on others it is just my two trainees and myself. Trainees work with me for three and a half years before taking their final exam in basket making. Some days I work completely alone. On those days I really find time to immerse myself in the basket I make. It is a kind of meditation. Feelings and emotions are often reflected in the baskets.

I will never fully complete my training as a basket maker. When looking at all the knowledge, all the techniques and variations available, it feels like I have only scratched the surface of this ancient craft. Since I started professionally in 2007, I have noticed a growing interest in basket making. In the courses I teach I have many participants, both newcomers and regulars. Making your own basket provides an excellent sense of achievement, which is I think what attracts people.

Willow has been grown for weaving and basket making for thousands of years. In Sweden, archaeologists discovered a fish trap made from willow, which dated over seven thousand years back. There are reasons to believe that willow was grown intentionally for weaving as early as that time. Our ancestors used willow for many purposes: in buildings and for boats, fishing tools, transportation, and storage. Items made from willow were necessities that disappeared with the introduction of plastic and other petrochemical materials. The history of basket making is something that is important to me – it is a real, honest, and local craft, representing knowledge, tradition, and pride.

WORKSPACE AND TOOLS

The barn where I live dates back to 1870. In the room where hay used to be stored as winter food for the animals, I have established my own workshop. It is a pleasing, spacious, and comfortable working area, which over the years has been filled with baskets in many shapes. I find great peace and creativity when staying here. Old buildings have their charm, and when the barn was renovated we were very focused on keeping as many of the old, original elements as possible. The most modern thing I have in the workshop is a heat pump to keep me warm during the cold Norwegian winter.

I have around two hundred square metres available for my workshop and storage. That is much more than is needed to start making baskets. All you need is a stool, a sharp knife, a good pair of scissors, an awl, and a metal rapper. An extra valuable asset is to have land available to grow your own willow.

The final thing required is knowledge – knowledge that must be passed on in order to prevent it from becoming lost.

PROCESS OVERVIEW

01 December to February is the time for harvesting willow. The weather determines when we harvest; if there is too much snow we wait. Twenty-five thousand willow cuttings will be cut, bundled, sorted into lengths, and re-bundled. It is hard, physical work. Two people are required for harvesting: one cuts the willow using a clearing saw while the other collects the cuttings.

02 When all the willow is cut, bundled, and driven back from the field, the ten different varieties of willow we grow here on the farm are stacked outdoors. The willow is then organized into lengths and all sticks with side shoots are sorted. There are many tons of willow and we spend several weeks carrying out the sorting. When the job is complete, the sense of joy is incredible. The result is a full stock of ten variations of beautifully finished, sorted willow that is ready to be dried before it can be soaked and prepared for weaving baskets.

03 For an oval basket, I often start with an underfoot base, which is made by standing on the base when making it in order to hold the sticks in place as you wrap and bend them. Sometimes, however, I create an oval base with a French variation, which is what is shown in image 03.

04 The next step is to insert the stakes – thirty-two pieces of willow that are attached into the base and form the vertical structure of the basket. This is important in achieving a smooth

03

05

04

06

07

08

and fine basket. The stakes are then bent upwards with the help of a knife.

05 Once the uprights have been pricked up and gathered towards the top, I use a three-rod waling technique to create a very strong weave that is required to give strength to the skeleton of the basket. This also ensures the gap between the stakes is equal.

06 The side of the basket can now be woven using randing. I use French randing, a system of weaving where one weaving rod crosses an upright each time. This involves selecting the same numbers of weaving rods as the uprights in the basket. There are different variations of randing that can be used. I choose depending on

the expression I want the basket to have and the basket's function.

07 Before creating the border I use four-rod waling to give the top of the basket strength. I then weave a "five-behind-two border". This border is named as such because you work with five pairs, and each standing stake is initially taken behind two others.

08 Once the border is complete, I add the handle. To do this, I place a thick piece of willow down through the border into the side. I then get two sets of four sticks of willow, which are as thick as uprights, twist them twice around the handle, and finish with a French knot.

FORGING A CAREER

The most common question that is asked when I tell people that I am a basket maker is whether it is possible to make a living from it. The next question is often what my "real" job is, as people assume that I am not a full-time basket maker. Many doubt that I can survive economically making baskets, and to be honest, I have had my doubts too. After over a decade of running a small company, I have not become rich but I live a rich life. I do what I love to do, and feel privileged to have my hobby and interest as my job and income.

Can you make a decent income by selling baskets alone? I would say that the answer is no. However there are things you can do to make a livelihood sustainable. I grow my own willow, and have twenty-five thousand cuttings. Along with my apprentices I harvest tons of willow every year, and much of this is then sold. In spring I make installations out of living willow. These are huts, tunnels, or fences for establishments such as preschools, parks, and private gardens. Some of these installations I maintain in the years after they are built. My most significant source of income is teaching and courses. These things, added together with creativity and a great amount of eagerness, mean that I am able to make a living from being a basket maker.

Activity follows the seasons, and no season is the same. In January it is quiet in terms of courses, but this is when we harvest, sort, and prepare willow. It is important to be resourceful in this profession and when living a sustainable lifestyle. Experiences from last year lead to improvements for the year ahead.

It is worth noting that when you have many ideas and multiple things that you want to do, it can be difficult to make everything happen due to the lack of time. Making a basket is time consuming. It takes from five hours for a plain basket to more than twenty for a complex one. I will never involve myself in any mass production as quality is very important to me. The requirements of running a business can be a constraint. I can't always do what I most want to do because I might have an order in for something else. Creativity blooms when I distance myself from constraints like these. However I must be structured in my work; there is no room for creativity and future ideas if routine tasks have piled up to take all my time. It would be a dream come true to have a month, or a year, engaging in a project without thinking about time or economy. That said, I love to be in charge of my time, even if that means working many hours when it is needed, and only being able to take time off in quiet periods.

Initially, marketing and the sale of baskets happened exclusively at fairs, markets, and directly from the workshop. After receiving inquiries about selling baskets online, I decided that I needed to set up an online shop. Marketing is now mainly done through social media. Facebook and Instagram are great platforms on which to showcase your work. Products, ideas, and events can be shared quickly and easily, and many of my inquiries come through social media now. The customer is able to directly get in touch with me, which is a great way to establish new relations, business ones or otherwise. It is more efficient and cost effective than traditional marketing. From time to time though, traditional media outlets spot that you are doing something unusual, and those articles and stories are important for visibility and marketing as well.

SURVIVING IN THE MODERN WORLD

Social media has also attracted interest from abroad, allowing me to sell baskets outside Norway. Living in a country where costs are high does mean that many may say that my baskets are expensive, especially in comparison with mass-produced baskets from low-cost countries. Sadly, rich countries' willingness to exploit poorer countries is probably the largest threat to the art of basket making. Everything seems to end up as a question of cost, and how can I compete on cost with workers in low-cost countries? When production takes place somewhere far away, when it is made invisible, we tend to forget the origin, and that someone made this basket. The basket no longer represents tradition, pride, knowledge, and craftsmanship. It becomes only another thing, in a country where everybody already has everything they need.

In our consumer culture, where cost is the focus, I try to move against the flow. Most products today are mass-produced and have no history. To me, basket making stands as something different: to know the origin of a product, what it is made from and by whom – to know the whole process of the product, from the field to marketplace – that makes it unique. Basket making may seem old fashioned and irrelevant to many. It is easy to think that technology has made it obsolete. The fact is though that there are no machines that make baskets.

The Norwegian traditions of basket making have been forgotten for a long time, and that in many ways gives room for using our own imagination and creativity. Many things can be made from willow. You can be traditional or experimental. I feel that I am a bit of both. In a tradition with such variation it takes years to find your own signature in the items made. This individuality is something that means basket making can survive in the modern world.

CONSERVING THE CRAFT AND ITS LIVELIHOOD

It is important to protect and maintain small endangered crafts like basket making as part of our cultural heritage. Traditional crafts are not only about the immediate usefulness of the items; as much as texts, music, drawings, and photography, knowledge of these crafts is part of our culture. Working as a basket maker is special and unique; there are so few of us. We have to keep protecting and promoting our knowledge and be proud keepers of the skills inherited through generations.

"Maybe it is the unpleasant fact that we are polluting our planet with plastic that raises the awareness for baskets"

There is a new era for baskets. You find them in trendy magazines, interior shops, and many other places. Unfortunately, most of them are mass produced, imported from low-cost countries, and far too often made by underpaid women and children. Basket making is somehow invisible today, but changes in society may make it more popular and relevant in the future. More and more people value locally made products, and the popularity of local craftsmanship seems to be on the rise. This is evidenced by the increasing number of people interested in basket-making courses. Maybe it is the unpleasant fact that we are polluting our planet with plastic that raises the awareness for baskets. Baskets can replace numerous plastic products, and many people today want to live in a more environmentally friendly way.

Pollution and climate change provide another motivation for me to continue weaving baskets and other useful products from local and natural materials. Only history will show if local, traditional crafts are a dream without a future or if they in fact represent a true vision of sustainability. Solid craftsmanship and the knowledge from small, endangered crafts deserve a place in our modern society.

There are many craftspeople who weave baskets, but Norway has only a few basket makers who hold a professional diploma. Due to Norway's outstretched topology, the distance between those involved in basket making is substantial. We do not meet regularly, and when we do it is often for courses. We have to continue to keep up quality standards and share knowledge. If we remain a small and highly competent group, I think society will continue to need us, now and in the future.

TRUG MAKING

Trugs are traditionally used in a farming or gardening context to harvest and sometimes store produce. They conjure up images of beautiful English countryside and cottage gardens, which is certainly a large part of their appeal. These days they symbolically capture a small part of the historical past while remaining a functional and reliable piece of equipment for avid gardeners; they also have the ability to add a rustic charm to any modern setting that is hard to resist.

"One and all seem to understand that this is not a simple money-harvesting operation but a living, growing branch of history being nurtured"

Tony Hitchcock

TONY HITCHCOCK

Golden Bay, New Zealand | trugmaker.co.nz

Training: Self-taught

Tony's workshop lies in an idyllic setting that is truly reflective of his craft and philosophy. With the help of his partner, Maddy, he has found a way to balance his part-time job as a forest ranger, looking after his family, and creating and selling something he loves. From planting the coppice trees to posting away the finished item, Tony brings together a wide range of skills to keep this traditional craft alive.

ORIGINS

I have always loved trees. Planting, tending, talking to – trees are an integral part of my existence. And to use the timber from a tree wisely, respectfully, has been a major ideal for me to strive towards.

My first job was in a forestry crew, felling large tracts of conifer forest. While this gave me many useful skills and a good work ethic, I felt it was a brutal, callous method, driven by big industry interested only in output and profit. By and by I found work as a forest ranger, building tracks and restoring historic timber cabins in our National Parks. Much of this restorative work was carried out with hand tools – an axe, adze, and chisel – employing the same techniques as the original builders.

When Brett Hutchinson, a good friend and longtime mentor, announced that he was retiring from a twenty-year-long career as trug maker, it seemed too good to be true that he would then go on to offer me the business, training included! Thus began my journey as a trug maker. The mainstay of the business is the traditional Sussex trug, and I also make Devon maunds and flower baskets. My partner Maddy takes care of the admin and accounts side of things, while our little boy Linden keeps us all busy.

MOTIVATIONS

I make trugs chiefly because I love making them. The processes of coppicing, steaming and bending, and assembling what at first glance seem to be flimsy pieces of wood in order to create something sturdy and robust – a functional item that will last a lifetime – all combine to give a pleasure not to be found in the hum-drum of nine-to-five jobs.

A trug is something you cannot make in a hurry, or assemble when your mind is elsewhere. It requires full concentration; a communication with the wood. Mindfulness would perhaps be the modern term. Each piece of timber behaves slightly differently under the drawknife or steamer, and if I wish to make a strong, aesthetically pleasing product, I must pick up on each and every subtlety. Small errors compound to affect the whole, but inversely, good judgement and attunement to the process result in something beautiful.

"To preach and lecture is one thing; to go out and plant, tend, and create speaks louder than words"

I find this concentration does not fatigue me as I assume it should. Perhaps this is because there is a meditative quality to the process and the absence of pressure to produce more and more stock in a shorter time. Very early on I found too high a turnaround to be counterproductive: as soon as I attempt to race ahead, the quality of my work diminishes rapidly.

There seems an increasing conscience of our effect on this planet's well-being and a desire to find alternatives. A useful item that is not plastic, not mass produced, and is made from local renewable resources creates a positive energy for prospective buyers. They are not just buying a trug; they are supporting change – a grassroots movement towards sustainability. And everyone I interact with, whether face to face or via email, loves the trug story: the story of a traditional craft being kept alive. One and all seem to understand that this is not a simple money-harvesting operation but a living, growing branch of history being nurtured.

A woodcraft such as this uses timber in a renewable fashion, making it a truly sustainable industry. Putting my energy into such a venture sits well in my conscience. The continual degradation of our landscapes is to me a crime and if using wood in a clean, renewable way inspires others to do the same, or at the very least see the trees around them as superb assets in every sense of the word, then some good has been done. To preach and lecture is one thing; to go out and plant, tend, and create speaks louder than words.

WORKSPACE AND TOOLS

My workshop is a small arch-roofed cabin built from locally grown and milled timber, tucked away down the back of a rambling garden. To reach it, I push-bike up the hedgerow-lined lane, cross an old swing bridge spanning the river, then weave through pastures fringed with stone fruit and fig trees. It is an enviable commute and puts me in a good frame of mind for the working day ahead.

The cabin is infused with a gentle scent of willow wood and sawdust. Centre stage is my Bodger's chair, or shaving horse, on which most of the forming and assembling of a trug is done. I have two home-built steamers for bending the wood (you can see one being used in the bottom-right photograph on the next page) and a razor-sharp drawknife that I use to carve the raw timber. An array of small hammers and pliers are laid out within easy reach. All have their specific job. A couple of light power drills are about the extent of modern tools here. It feels an unobtrusive space and not at all industrial.

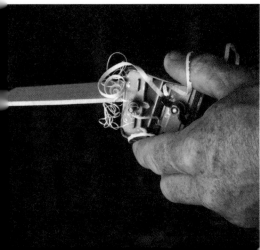

PROCESS OVERVIEW

01 A trug is comprised of seven aspen poplar slats steam-bent into a willow or hazel rim. A willow or hazel hoop handle is fixed outside the rim and slats. Two poplar feet are fixed to the keel slat and cut in a way to allow the trug to sit level. In winter, good, straight stems of cricket-bat willow or hazel are selected for coppicing. These need to have reasonably straight grain and be free of defects. I cut using a sharp folding handsaw.

02 Back at the workshop, I use a froe to cleave the stems into quarters, and a billhook to remove excess wood. Then I dress each quarter with the drawknife. These will become the rims and handles of trugs. By harvesting in winter the bark does not peel away, giving a protective cap as well as a really good visual effect.

03 The dressed lengths go into the long cylindrical steamer until they are malleable enough to bend around the "forms", which, when pegged and wedged, hold the timber into the shape of a trug rim or handle. This is a busy time, as once the wood is harvested, the time between steaming and forming cannot be too far apart.

04 After several months drying, I select a good shape and colour match, remove a rim and handle from their forms, and fix together with copper nails. This provides the basic frame.

05 Next, pieces of aspen poplar bandsawed down to just a few millimetres thick are selected for the boards. All must have a bevel hand-planed down their edges and their flats drawknived smooth.

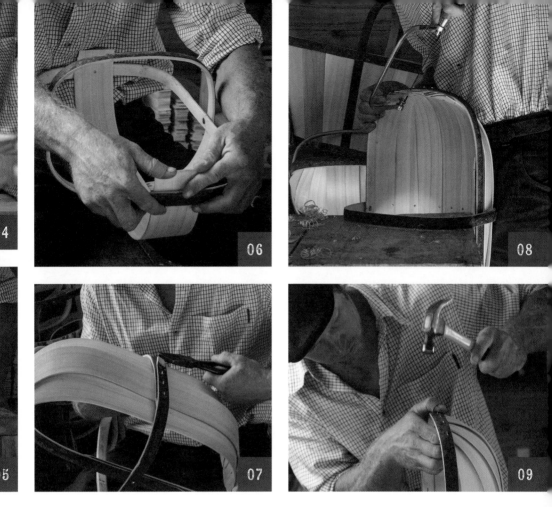

The drawknife is also used to shave off the corners where the boards will overlap each other.

06 Starting with the "keel" or centreboard, each slat is steamed and bent to shape over my knee. This process asks for complete focus and the ability to "read" the tension in the wood, all the while working fast enough so the effect of the steam does not wear off. Brute force or inattention here will waste much timber.

07 Working out from the keel board, each of the seven slats are steamed, bent, moulded into the trug frame, and fixed with rose-head copper nails. Good, even curves that mirror one another are necessary for making a strong,

visually appealing trug. I constantly check for conformity as I go.

08 When all the slats are in place, I trim the tag ends off with a coping saw, slice off the tooth marks with a small, sharp knife, and then flatten all the nails to a tidy finish.

09 Lastly, the feet are fixed on. I pre-cut aspen feet on the bandsaw, arras the edges with a pocket knife, and fix with larger copper nails. Great care is taken at this point as a missed hit with the hammer can scar the still soft wood and spoil all my previous work. A last tidy up with some fine grit sandpaper and the trug is set away to dry for two or three weeks before sale.

FORGING A CAREER

Trug making is a part-time venture for us. It dovetails in around my work as a forest ranger and family commitments. This can be difficult at times – there is no point in glossing over the awkward points of this lifestyle choice. Trugs sell sporadically, generally with a spike of orders in the period leading up to Christmas (which is in the summer months in New Zealand). There is a real challenge for us to budget throughout the year. My wage work provides stability. As any self-employed person will tell you, nobody pays for sick days, training days, or annual leave when you work for yourself. It is hard to accurately calculate the number of hours spent making a trug or maund, especially when you take into account all aspects of the process, from tending the coppice plots to packaging the finished item and shipping it away. We don't want to price ourselves out of the market but need to make a living wage for this venture to be truly sustainable.

Of invaluable service is my partner Maddy, who looks after the administration side of things. If the accounts are not shipshape, the invoices not correct, the tax not dealt with, then it would matter little how good a product I am able to produce, for it would not be long before the whole venture collapsed.

"Word of mouth plays a subtle yet powerful role in promoting our product"

Around ninety per cent of our trugs are sold online, through our website. Most sales are within the country, though we can sell overseas. Some countries have stringent import regulations on items such as untreated wood, which restricts us somewhat. Advertising is essential, although for glossy magazine adverts, the cost can be almost prohibitive. Word of mouth plays a subtle yet powerful role in promoting our product. We take great pains to treat each and every customer with respect and warmth. In a world where we increasingly buy items through online retailers, many communications are with a computer programme's automated response. We endeavour to be the antithesis to that. Even via email, the tone of one's voice can seep through the typed words.

For anybody considering a craft like trug making as a business venture, I would say the single most important factor is passion for the craft. A deep love for the craft will bridge many gulfs, whereas if your starting point is a desire to make lots of money, or latching on to a passing whimsy in the hope that it will lead to some bucolic idyll, prepare to be disappointed.

SURVIVING IN THE MODERN WORLD

With a business like trug making, I must always be thinking at least a year ahead. If I do not have a good stock of components drying for next year, then I will run into trouble later. The same applies to keeping our brand and story fresh and applicable. Technology and social media are moving at such a pace that it can become overwhelming to even try to keep apace with it all.

We inherited this business from a man who sold most of his stock via telephone, mail order, or people on craft trails. Now, there seems a myriad of ways to promote and sell your product. We are still investigating many of these avenues. Rather than embarking upon a social media onslaught, we are asking ourselves what will actually be applicable to our ethos. Above all, we wish to keep that – I hesitate to say "old-fashioned" – rapport with potential customers.

Time is perhaps the most constricting factor for me in terms of building trugs. All of us live such busy lives that it is often a struggle to delegate time to do all we want and feel bound to do. Having a young family is the greatest blessing for us but it also takes an enormous amount of time, energy, and money. A more financially secure option for me would be solid wage work, and Maddy and I have often talked to this end. Juggling part-time work with a craft business is a challenge but we are both confident that given due patience all will even out, provided we continue to make decisions based on healthy outcomes rather than amassing wealth.

I think the main threat to our craft business would be economic downturn. A trug is an item that people want, rather than need. In times of austerity, it could well become harder to sell trugs in healthy numbers.

CONSERVING THE CRAFT AND ITS LIVELIHOOD

In bygone days, trugs were made out in the woods entirely from hand tools. The woodsman lived in the woods. Today, a mixture of hand tools and machines are used, saving time, labour, and lessening the wastage of wood. I suppose the really modern trug or maund would be a plastic bucket. Hypothetically, I could buy an industrial complex and churn out thousands of plastic buckets a day, sell in bulk to hardware stores, and watch the profits roll in.

Of course, this misses the point of a trug and why they still exist. People love them and you don't have to buy a new one every few months when the current one breaks. Crafts like trug making offer an alternative to cheap, shoddy junk. But further than that, a trug is more than just a trug; as mentioned earlier, it is history breathing; it is heritage. There is something quintessentially English about trugs, evocative of hedgerows, thatched cottages, and walled gardens. To find a trug only within the confines of a stuffy museum would be a crying shame. The trug my mother uses daily is a facsimile of what her great, great grandmother would have gathered her carrots in. The maund our neighbour uses to pick apples into is no different to what their forefathers would have used in the harvest six or seven generations ago. This is too precious to lose.

Having been tutored by Brett on trug and maund making, using the same tools he used – and slowly realizing just how rich was his store of experience, information, and knowledge – has been a journey of incalculable wealth for me. It has been obvious, too, the joy this has given Brett to have been able to pass trug craft on to the next generation. In continuity, his life's work is honoured.

Humans have a deep need to feel they are a useful part of society. Using one's hands and crafting something useful enables that. And being part of a legacy passed down and down through the generations gives a rich, strong sense of the tapestry of life. To share and pass all this on – I would not have it any other way.

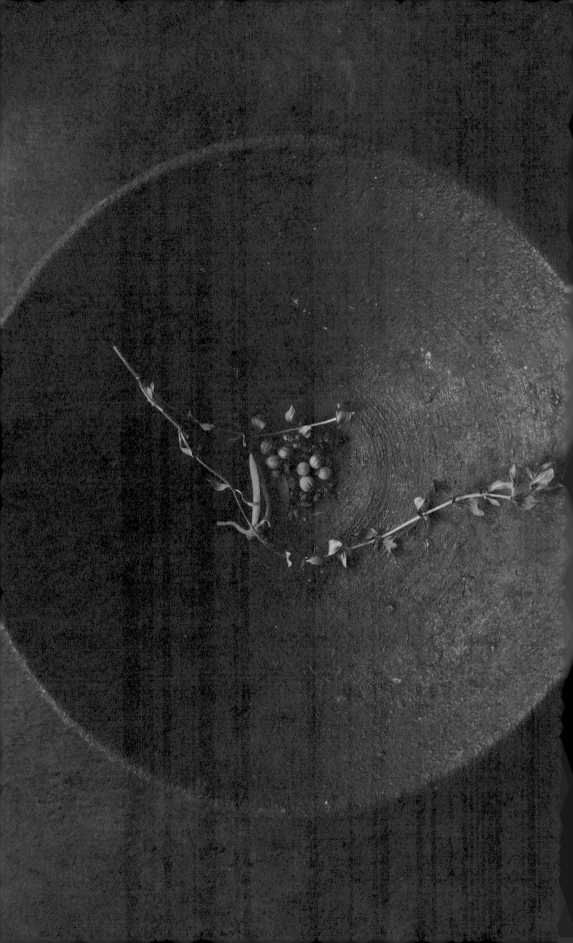

POTTERY

Pottery techniques such as slab-building and coil-building have been used
to craft objects by hand since before the advent of the potter's wheel. Coil-
building involves the vessel being built up by adding coils of clay on top of
each other, allowing a variety of tall and bulbous shapes to be created with
a strong structure. In slab-building the vessel is shaped from a smooth slab
of flattened clay, enabling you to create unique features and angular forms
which are difficult to achieve with other pottery methods. Wheel-throwing
is another common technique and what typically comes to mind when
thinking of pottery: a piece of clay is placed on a pottery wheel and the
potter moulds the clay as the wheel rotates. What all these methodologies
have in common – and one of the reasons so many people are drawn to
these time-honoured traditions – is the direct connection the creator gets
with the natural material.

"In its ability to allow humans to store
and transport food, seeds, and water, the
vessel has had a profound impact on the
development of many civilizations"

Mitch Iburg

MITCH IBURG

Minnesota, USA | mitchiburg.com

Training: BA in Fine Art at Coe College + Self-taught

Mitch Iburg's ceramic work is centred on the use of natural clay, which he gathers himself, and each piece's process is heavily informed by these materials and the unique geology of their local region. Mitch gained a BA in Fine Art in 2011, and has since held multiple artist residencies. He has also been featured in exhibitions in the US and abroad.

ORIGINS

While pursuing undergraduate studies I became fascinated with Japanese ceramic vessels produced from the eighth to the sixteenth century CE. Their crude forms and austere surfaces both challenged my previous conceptions of ceramic art and helped me to articulate the qualities I sought in my own work.

Although shaped by hand, these works retained strong expressions of the earth from which they were made. By using local unrefined clays, early potters unknowingly captured the unique attributes of their regional geology. Additionally, their use of wood-burning kilns allowed them to fire to temperatures at which elements found in wood ash flux and form a natural glaze – expanding this geographical record to reflect the diversity of their forests.

This ability for the vessel to act as a shared expression for place, material, and maker became a core inspiration in my practice and fuelled my desire to travel throughout the country to work closely with locally available resources. Despite each region yielding different materials, the consistent pursuit of utilitarian ideas has helped to unify my work throughout my career. Although I have worked separately with purely sculptural works, maintaining the context of vessel making, whether traditional or progressive, has been important in defining my artistic identity.

MOTIVATIONS

Working with clays and minerals harvested from the ground is by no means a practical endeavour. The time spent researching, locating, transporting, and testing materials easily outweighs the time spent actively making objects. Despite these challenges, working directly with natural resources allows me to promote the expressions and attributes inherent to a specific region in a way that using commercially mined clays cannot.

Knowing the exact sources of my materials and the immense history through which they have been shaped, I feel a great responsibility to create work that honours them and their place of origin. This occurs in two main ways: first, by subjecting clays to as little processing and alteration as possible in order to maintain their original character. Second, by exploring forms, developing recipes, and using construction methods inspired by the region's natural history and geographical expressions. As I have worked in many different regions, upholding this goal while living a semi-nomadic lifestyle has forced me to adjust my approaches and recipes to accurately reflect the new conditions of each location.

"I recognize a growing presence of contemporary clay artists showing the same dedication to using local materials within the vessel-making genre"

Pursuing this endeavour within conventional craft and utilitarian traditions comes with many challenges, as most of my materials have low plasticity (how easy or difficult it is to mould it), high organic matter, and varying contaminations of sand and stone. Often, these characteristics translate into a very narrow range of working properties, firing temperatures, and functional applications. Rather than altering these deposits to suit my demands, I have developed distinct bodies of work which balance material attributes with artistic intent. Clay bodies composed of fine-grained plastic clays are used in the formation of wheel-thrown tableware, while those made of coarse, refractory clays are used for hand-built sculptural vessels.

Working with divergent methods and ideas allows me to continuously uphold a primary goal of maintaining honesty to material and place while exploring a broad range of ideas related to clay and its connection to history. While this material-forward approach can be seen as diverging from the early traditions in which it is rooted, I recognize a growing presence of contemporary clay artists showing the same dedication to using local materials within the vessel-making genre. On a global scale, this work is quickly gaining widespread interest and is providing artists with a platform for expression that is capable of bridging the gap between traditional craft and contemporary practices.

WORKSPACE AND TOOLS

My current studio is located within a historic industrial building in urban Saint Paul, Minnesota. I share this space with my partner and fellow ceramic artist, Zoë Powell. Aside from a space for making, the studio serves as a location where we are able to store and process all materials for our clay bodies.

Having worked in rural environments throughout much of my career, the transition to an urban setting has created an exciting contrast to the conventional lifestyle typically associated with the ceramic artist. While I recognize my roots in a historical media, working within this space forces me to re-address the role of my studio practice and identity in a modern time.

The relatively small studio can be converted to accommodate the work tasks at hand. Shelving units are wall-mounted to allow maximum floor space for clay storage and screening. Crude and processed clays are stored in large movable bins which slide beneath the counter space. At any given time, this counter space may be used for working on hand-built pieces, drying clays, or displaying finished work. After making, all work is transported to separate facilities where it is fired in electric or wood-burning kilns.

PROCESS OVERVIEW

01 My process begins by researching geological maps, soil surveys, and historical mining records. These resources lead me to areas where deposits of clay or minerals are likely to be found. I seek and collect samples of many materials from different regions throughout Minnesota, taking detailed notes of their location, purity, and abundance.

02 Before mixing large batches of clay, each sample is tested for plasticity, shrinkage, durability, and absorption after being fired. These results ultimately determine the material's future application in either sculpture or throwing clay bodies. During this testing stage I examine materials on their own and blended together to achieve a wider range of variations.

03 Many clays must be screened to remove large stones and organic matter. Crude clay is rehydrated and mixed with water before being filtered to a desired mesh size. Screened sand and stones are often added to another recipe or crushed and used as a glaze ingredient. The remaining slurry is dried in plaster troughs until the desired consistency is reached.

04 Often, multiple clays are blended together to achieve a clay body that meets specific demands for workability, colour, or firing range. (The firing range is a temperature range at which the clay will be successful – too cool and the clay will remain porous, too hot and it will begin to melt. Each clay has a different temperature range.) For this high-fire clay body, two fine-

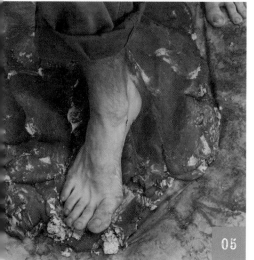

grained, iron-rich clays are mixed with coarse, refractory kaolin. When mixed together, these clays will be able to withstand temperatures exceeding 2300°F.

05 To maximize efficiency, several firings' worth of clay is prepared at one time. Clays are blended directly on the studio floor until homogenous using foot-wedging techniques. Often, additional crushed stones and aggregates will be added at this stage for additional strength, texture, and visual contrast after firing.

06 While various forming techniques are used depending on the specific properties of the clay, coil-building methods are exclusively used to make sculptural wood-fired work. This method allows me to personalize historical hand-building techniques by using clay strata to reference the geological expressions of sedimentary rock structures present in the landscapes where I have worked.

07 After drying, most work is carefully transported and loaded into the wood kiln where it will be fired for four days with a mix of hard and soft woods. Over the firing's duration, accumulated wood ash and charcoal melts to form a natural glaze where temperatures exceed 2300°F. No applied glazes are used on the surfaces of this work. The process continues on the next page.

08 Temperature is strategically controlled by carefully monitoring the conditions of the kiln. Timing of stokes is established by observing the colour and movement of flame, the amount of smoke, and the charcoal accumulation within the kiln. Many factors influence the surfaces and colours of the final work, including peak temperature, wood species, clay composition, and stacking arrangement.

09 Massive hardwood charcoal beds accumulate over the four-day firing. These embers maintain heat and encourage a slow cooling cycle – an essential factor in achieving the matte, stone-like surfaces sought in this body of work. After seven days of natural cooling, the kiln door is un-bricked, the remaining charcoal is shovelled out, and all the work is unloaded.

10 Many pieces are strategically loaded directly on the floor of the kiln where they become buried in charcoal and develop heavily ember-encrusted surfaces. After unloading, each piece must be carefully sanded using varying grits of diamond polishing pads to remove sharp fragments of unmelted ash and fragile sintered embers.

FORGING A CAREER

Working in such a labour-intensive medium requires careful balancing of the numerous tasks that make up my work cycle. To maintain predictability within this workflow, my annual schedule is adapted to the seasons. Clay prospering must occur between April and late October to avoid the region's harsh winter conditions. During this time I must collect enough material to meet the demands of the year's upcoming sales and exhibitions. These materials are kept in the studio and are processed throughout the year.

Firings in the wood kiln must happen during a similar time frame. Often occurring once in the spring and once in the fall, these set events encourage a natural rhythm of production that increases as the firing date approaches and slows after it is complete. Although infrequent, each firing yields roughly five to six months' worth of inventory.

While the varied colour palettes and heavily textured surfaces achieved in the wood kiln best complement sculptural work, certain forms and wheel-thrown tableware are fired in the electric kiln to achieve quieter surfaces with greater predictability. Because of the availability of this firing method throughout the year, I can produce custom work in relatively short periods of time. This flexibility has been especially helpful in meeting the demands of restaurants, who often have strict requirements and time frames.

Nearly all production slows in the winter months. During this period I spend most of my time planning for exhibitions, writing, distributing work to galleries, and preparing for online sales. While all of the studio tasks must be properly balanced, this period of office work is crucial in my ability to maintain a living as a working artist.

Revenue from my online store generates roughly two-thirds of my annual income. Managing my own sales requires keeping detailed inventory catalogues and numerous photographs of each piece to be sold. To supplement this income, I have maintained healthy relationships with galleries throughout the US and abroad. Each venue promotes the work within a regional niche market, but more importantly provides exposure for the work's ideas and context within the greater art world. A relatively new addition to my studio output has been collaborating with chefs and restaurants on lines of custom tableware. I work closely with these clients in designing works that both conform to and challenge the conventional dining experience, while maintaining an element of my own identity and approach to material.

SURVIVING IN THE MODERN WORLD

Craft is especially valuable in contemporary society due to its ability to connect the viewer to a way of life that many forms of modern artistic expression cannot. In addition to recording evidence of how people lived and how they responded to their surroundings, folk traditions give an especially intimate look into the ways cultures passed on the values of their work and the craftsmanship with which it was created.

While this transference of ideas and techniques to future generations is crucial to craft's identity, it presents many challenges over time. As civilizations evolve, demand for traditionally made objects may decrease, or supply of conventional resources may become extinguished. In response, artisans must adapt the ways of the past to fit the contexts of their own time.

In search of my own relevance, I attempt to examine historical practices within the global context of the contemporary art world, and also through the local context of my natural environment. My wheel-thrown tableware continues the legacy of providing handmade objects for food and kitchen use. With this work I strive to balance contemporary aesthetics with a reference to the first domestic wares made by human hands thousands of years ago.

Artistic content is not the only aspect that must conform to modern times. As both an artist and a business owner, I embrace the use of digital technology and communication as a resource for improving marketing and sales. Instagram in particular has acted as a strong catalyst for the development of numerous relationships with galleries and restaurants – many of which I continue to work with to this day.

Social media also allows me to share elements of my creative process that are unseen in the finished work. By presenting photographs of the sources of my materials and their place within the environment, I am able to further articulate the natural expressions of place in which my work is rooted.

CONSERVING THE CRAFT AND ITS LIVELIHOOD

In its ability to allow humans to store and transport food, seeds, and water, the vessel has had a profound impact on the development of many civilizations. Furthermore, the presence of domestic clay objects in religious, ceremonial, and political contexts throughout time has allowed for something as simple as shaped and fired earth to assume its contemporary status as a culturally significant media.

In a time when young individuals are expressing decreasing interest in folk traditions and academic institutions are slowly replacing craft curricula with technology-based art forms, many express fear for the future of the medium. Additionally, there is belief that veering far from its original context will ultimately jeopardize our ability to maintain artistic literacy in traditional lineages, and as a result, fail to provide an accurate record of history for the future. While I believe it is inevitable that integration into the fine art world will encourage new and progressive applications, craft's relevance within the context of human civilization will allow it to continue as a field of exploration as long as artists are willing to carry its history.

Although I currently do not work with assistants or apprentices, I hope that by exhibiting, writing, and sharing information about the context of my work, my efforts may inspire others to develop their own unique adaptations of a given lineage or tradition. I also hope to promote the importance of experimentation, without which I could not have established my own voice. By critically revisioning the ways of the past, taking risks, and assessing failures, I have chosen which of history's components require conformity and which must be rejected to arrive at personal expression. Above all, I believe this encouragement to define one's ideas within the expanse of history is one of the greatest benefits of working in craft-based media.

SARAH PIKE

British Columbia, Canada | sarahpikepottery.com

Training: Alberta College of Art & Design + University of Colorado Boulder +
University of Minnesota

Sarah Pike is a potter based in the idyllic mountains of British Columbia, Canada. Having harboured a passion for clay from a young age, she is now a full-time artisan specializing in slab-building items such as mugs and teapots, and shares her expertise through frequent exhibitions and workshops. Her wares combine everyday function with the irregular charm of the uniquely hand-built, and have found a devoted audience among ceramics enthusiasts.

ORIGINS

I grew up in a home and community of artists and craftspeople. My mother wove baskets and worked in fibre, and my dad worked in wood, glass, and stone. They were part-time urban homesteaders, growing food, and building the items we needed, but also working jobs to pay the bills. I spent my childhood playing outdoors and making things, surrounded by that creative activity. I was fortunate to have parents who encouraged my artistic pursuits from a young age. My sister and I spent many afternoons in our local art centre, attending a variety of art classes, including clay sculpting – my favourite.

Then, in my early teens, we moved to an island off the west coast of Canada and I bought my first kiln. I was working at a restaurant part-time through the summer, and spent my savings on an old, used electric kiln. It seems strange now, but it was a natural progression to buy a kiln at thirteen years old. I made little slab- and coil-built items in our basement, and fired them in that little old kiln. Later, I went to art school with plans to major in painting or drawing, but one elective class in ceramics quickly rekindled my love for clay.

MOTIVATIONS

I remember the first mug I made in art school. It was small, rough, and heavy. As I sipped tea from its thick rim, and wrapped my hands around its squat form – a shape I had squeezed out of a soft lump of clay – I was blown away by the material and its potential. Despite the fact that I had already played with clay for many years, the function of this object took clay to another level. Suddenly, the object I was making had an intrinsic tie to this intimate experience after its completion; the sensual and compelling holding, touching, and nourishing aspect of pottery. I had always been attracted to clay for its tactility and malleability, its earthy smell, and its raw connection to the natural world, but now there was a connection to the senses through the finished piece's intended use: the holding and serving of tasty, aromatic food and drink.

I am a maker of things, but like most makers, I am also a collector of handmade things. Our cupboards are home to many pots by many different potters, showcasing different styles and techniques. As time goes by, this collection has grown and expanded to include other crafts: hand-carved wooden spoons, hand-woven brooms, forged tools for the wood stove, handmade quilts and clothes, leather work, blown glass, and wood furniture to name a few. These pieces, often made by friends and acquaintances from a wide community of craftspeople, are so incredibly special to me. They enrich the experience in which I use them on a daily basis. I love that their design and fabrication came from the hard work and skill of human hands. I love being a part of this fabric of craft. I love hearing from customers that their morning coffee tastes better in one of my mugs. For me, making and using handcrafted objects is a quiet resistance to the mass-produced, disposable consumer culture.

WORKSPACE AND TOOLS

My family and I live on an acre of land on the edge of a little ski town in the Rocky Mountains. A few years ago we built a garage-style building with windows all down one side. I can look out of those windows and see the mountains and trees change through the seasons. The natural light, the surroundings, and beautiful workspace inspire me to get in the studio every day. In fact, when I walk into my studio in the morning, I still stop, sigh, and say, "Oh, hello studio!" with my heart expanding and a smile on my lips.

I make all my work at the table, not on a pottery wheel, so the space is designed to hold two long tables that I can walk around as I work. They are both beautifully solid tables built by my dad, one covered with canvas and one with cement. All my work begins with a solid table, a rolling pin, and a soft lump of clay. The clay comes from Plainsman Clays, a company based four hours' drive away who mine the clay locally.

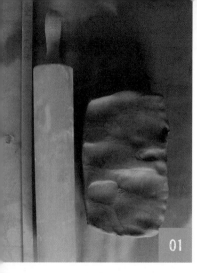

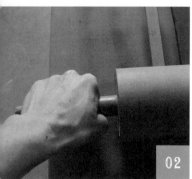

PROCESS OVERVIEW

01 I begin my day by dampening my canvas-covered table with a wet sponge. I prepare my clay by wedging it to remove any air bubbles and even out its consistency. I then pound my clay into a rectangular lump.

02 Next, I throw and roll out the soft clay into a large, rectangular slab a quarter of an inch thick. Wooden slats and a rolling pin help create an even thickness.

03 I smooth and compress the surface with a rubber rib to both clean up the surface and strengthen the slab as a whole.

04 Next, I cut the slab into my desired shapes. This is reminiscent of cutting fabric from a pattern, or cookies from rolled-out dough. Once cut, I flip the slab pieces onto the cement table

and smooth and compress their other side. The cement table is smooth and absorbent, and quickly stiffens one face of the slab, just enough to make the slab workable for construction.

05 While the slab is sitting on the cement, I texture the slabs with hand-carved texture tools. I make these tools out of wet clay, refining them as they dry. Once satisfied, they are bisqued (heated up to bisque temperature – I use 998°C or 1828°F) for permanence. I use both stamps and rollers. My texture is primarily about relief, but the recessed mark is important too and both are considered in the design. I push or roll the various textures into the clay.

06 Once the slabs are textured and slightly stiffened, I can bend and stretch them into the desired forms. I join the seams by brushing

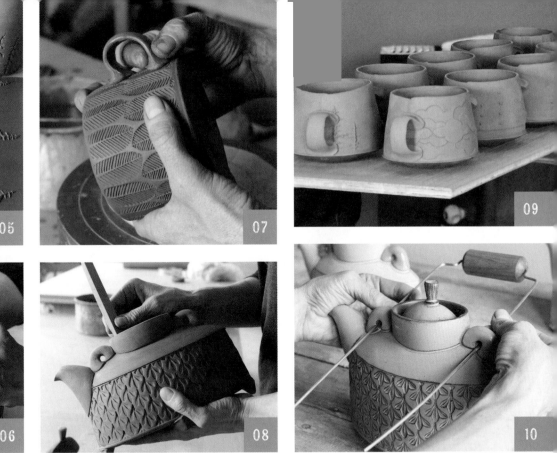

water onto the cut edge, and then by roughing up that edge with a serrated tool. I compress the join with my fingers and a piece of wood.

07 As the clay stiffens, I can add more components such as handles, spouts, lids, and knobs. Ideally, the form is only just stiff enough for this step. The softer I can work the clay, the lower the chance of cracks and warping, but if it is too soft, the form will collapse and I must wedge up my clay to start again.

08 It is important to dry slab-built pots slowly, checking to make sure no warping or cracking occurs along the way. During this process, I make any needed refinements, such as cleaning up seams with a metal rib or rubber pointed tool. This both compresses the join and accentuates it. Light plastic covers the pots to slow the drying.

09 When the pots are bone dry, I load them into the kiln and slowly fire them to bisque temperature. This firing removes the chemically combined water. After this firing, clay will no longer slake down (break down and become malleable again) when submerged in water. Once cool, I wipe the pots with a damp sponge to remove dust, and then dip them in glaze. Next, I load the pots into the kiln and fire them to their final temperature.

10 Once cooled, I attach any post-firing components such as wood and wire handles to teapots. I enjoy this multi-media part of the process. I turn, drill, and sand the wood, thread the wire through the wood, and finish by bending the wire into the desired shape with pliers. The wood adds a soft touch to the clay and is reminiscent of antique tinware buckets and oil cans.

FORGING A CAREER

When I first considered a career as a craftsperson, it was not a new story to me. When I imagined what my life would look like as a potter, it was a simple one: a studio, a work table, and a community that supported me. The reality is a little more complicated. As with anything, the balance is tricky to find.

Currently seventy-five per cent of my income comes from pottery sales, and twenty-five per cent of my income comes from teaching workshops. My time is allocated quite differently. I spend a good deal of time in the studio, but I also spend a lot of time at my computer, updating my website and social media feeds, responding to emails, and organizing sales, exhibitions, and workshops. I also spend a good chunk of time packing pots for shipment. Some days I make pots for ten to twelve hours, and other days for only three. Some days I am travelling to workshops or shows. There is not really a weekend, but I can take a few hours here and there as I please.

"My kids are growing up fast, there are mountain adventures calling, and friends to see and chat with. These things sustain me and inspire my studio practice, so they are essential to my career"

In the beginning I was continuously seeking opportunity, and now I am struggling to know what opportunities to say "yes" to, and which ones to decline. The balance of work, family and social life, and health is a difficult one to navigate. My kids are growing up fast, there are mountain adventures calling, and friends to see and chat with. These things sustain me and inspire my studio practice, so they are essential to my career. Because of this, I've had to learn how to say "no", which can be a difficult thing to do.

These days, the studio is always busy, but I make an effort to carve out time to design and test new forms, textures, and finishes. A lot of these tests result in failures, so can be hard to justify, but they are necessary to keep the work, and my engagement in the work, from stagnating. These exploration days are also fun days in the studio because I am excited to try out new ideas and work through the challenges of a design from start to finish. That said, there is an element of this in every pot I make. I believe this is the innate character of craftspeople. We continually endeavour to hone our skills and improve our designs, both in function and aesthetic.

SURVIVING IN THE MODERN WORLD

Social media has been a huge asset to me. It has helped me get my name and work out to a large audience. It has also given me access to an ever-growing global community of makers. I love to see what a friend of mine is doing in her studio in Australia, or what another friend in Vancouver is making. The story behind their crafted object expands as I learn about their interests and what inspires them. Little glimpses into other makers' lives connect me to their work in such a real way. It is something like the traditional village potter, but on a global scale.

> "I kind of love that I make work through an ancient craft, but use my smartphone to post the work on my website, promote it on social media... It is paradoxical, but beautiful"

I imagine that the current trend of valuing the handmade object will change and evolve. I'm not sure what that will look like, but craft has been around for millennia; I feel confident it will persevere, and so will our connection to it. Perhaps this connection will even deepen in response to the digital age, or perhaps craft and the digital will simply evolve together. I kind of love that I make work through an ancient craft, but use my smartphone to post the work on my website, promote it on social media, and sell it to someone in Denmark, Australia, or Texas. It is paradoxical, but beautiful.

CONSERVING THE CRAFT AND ITS LIVELIHOOD

I don't see any decline in humans' need to make things with their hands. My kids have smartphones, but my daughter is currently carving a wooden spoon and fork from some scraps of wood her grandpa gave her. She also makes pots, paints, beads, and folds origami. You would have a hard time stopping her. YouTube is full of hugely popular DIY videos because people love projects. We just can't stop making things.

I recognize that I am living in a time and place that values the handcrafted. Sometimes as a maker, living in a little mountain town, I realize that I might be living in a bubble. I also recognize that there are similar bubbles all around the world, and social media and the internet connects us. When I first saw 3D printers and 3D computer design software, my heart imploded because it felt like the end of craft. Now I see it as simply another tool in the craftsperson's toolbox. It may not be in mine, but neither is a pottery wheel – and I make pottery!

I have huge respect for a well-crafted object. It inspires me to spend the time working out the details; to make each motion in my process economical in time, movement, and appearance; to find that elusive balance between the overworked and overlooked; to make work that is both a pleasure to look at and to use. I stress the importance of questioning these things when I teach workshops – the how and why we are doing each step of the process. In a time when so many things are made to fall apart and be discarded, we have this beautiful opportunity to take the time with the things we make. Let's celebrate the work and skills of our hands. As humans, we make things that can last a lot longer than our own lives. They can be plastic, sitting for eternity in a landfill, or crafted from natural materials, celebrated, and possibly handed down through generations. Let's strive to craft our objects well.

BROOM MAKING

To many, a broom may seem a mundane object that sits at the back of the cupboard until needed. Like the other items in this book though they represent a small piece of socio-cultural and economic history. They come in various forms depending on their origin and purpose, and have held a strong position in supernatural beliefs as early as the fifteenth century as a mode of transport for witches. A broom's simplicity can also be something of beauty, handcrafted by securing pieces of harvested broomcorn around a handle and requiring an incredible amount of dexterity on the part of the maker.

"It is vital that I share my art with as many people as possible. Not only so that the art of broom making exists, but so that it also thrives"

Justin D. Burton

JUSTIN D. BURTON

Kansas, USA | thebroomhouse.com

Training: On-the-job training with Christopher Robbins

Justin has made it his aim to raise broom making's profile beyond that as something purely functional but as an art in its own right. A proponent of the importance of preserving heritage crafts, Justin teaches broom making at a local college and his own workshop. He also looks to make his workmanship more sustainable, using only natural materials and aiming to grow his own broomcorn. The use of solely natural materials ensures his brooms are stronger and longer-lasting than synthetic alternatives; these properties, in conjunction with Justin's individual designs, mean that his brooms can also be considered heirloom pieces.

ORIGINS

I must confess that I was not always the most artistically inclined. I did not consider myself someone to have a grasp of what craftsmanship was or a clue about art in general. I would not have comprehended that my life would revolve around art and crafts because of the seemingly lowly broom. I discovered the art of broom making while attending Berea College in Kentucky. Every student there is required to have a job for the college. My job was initially in printing services so, combined with writing papers, my life was nothing but paper. I felt overwhelmed by the academic side of college and wanted to do something with my hands. It was then that I discovered that the college had a broom shop I could work for. It is something that was unusual and very physically demanding, so it caught my eye. I quickly fell in love with broom making and have been attempting to master it ever since.

MOTIVATIONS

I love to make brooms. It allows me to interact with people throughout the world who would otherwise have never seen a broom as beautiful. I meet a person who sees one of my brooms and gets excited about all the possibilities of brooms almost every week. Broom making has pushed me to see where I can take the craft. No one has really pushed the boundaries of what a broom can be, and I hope to be that person. It helps that people seem more aware of artisan brooms in recent years, and more and more people are rediscovering them. It is also becoming easier for people who make brooms to connect. I talk online with broom makers who are just starting out and give them advice. It makes me happy to see younger people starting to make brooms as a hobby or a side business.

"I see broom making as a Zen-like experience. It allows to me focus on the moment of making, so I am forced to focus on the now"

The history of broom making has actually become an issue for my business to a large extent. People's perceptions of brooms and broom making are derived from the nineteenth century. That is not what I am trying to do. Attempting new things and discovering opportunities a traditional broom maker would not try gives me a great deal of motivation. In a weird way, the history of my craft inspires me to be bold and do what would have been crazy a hundred years ago. There is a clear divide in the community of broom makers as to how they are focusing their efforts. The younger generation, including myself, are trying to be bolder. Many of the older generation (but not all!) are set in their ways or want to make brooms because it is a traditional craft. There is nothing wrong with that; it is just a different interpretation of what it means to make brooms.

I see broom making as a Zen-like experience. It allows to me focus on the moment of making, so I am forced to focus on the now. When making, you have to be in the present or you might make a mistake that will ruin your creation. Making brooms is part of how I relieve stress and I find that I am more anxious if I go a few weeks without making brooms.

WORKSPACE AND TOOLS

I maintain my workshop in production mode – it takes a lot of effort to make brooms as a living, so it needs to be done efficiently. I also keep brooms and clippings related to brooms and myself on the walls. It helps me draw inspiration from my own past achievements, as well as those of others.

My broom knife and hammer are my most-used tools. They are specialized tools for making brooms and have been developed over hundreds of years. They are still relatively easy to get hold of compared to some of my equipment, which is not something really made anymore. You have to have a lot of luck to find it at reasonable prices. Because of the equipment's age, nearly every piece has a story behind it. My main pieces are my tying table and broom winder. My tying table was acquired from a man who had it in a barn for many years. My broom winder came from Richard Henson of Kentucky. He passed away and no one in his family was able to take over his shop. Every broom I make on his machine helps to keep his family's legacy of excellent brooms alive.

Depending on the type of broom you are making, you can either use string or wire to tie the broom together. A tying table uses string and is basically a table that has a wheel where the string is located. While making a broom, you press down on the wheel with your foot to control how much tension the broom has. I use my tying table mostly for small brooms, brooms with crooked handles, and for braiding brooms. A broom winder is a device developed in the nineteenth century to create full-size brooms. The kick wheel (a wheel again powered by the foot) turns the handle to attach the metal wire while broomcorn is added.

The broomcorn I use at the moment is sourced from Mexico, although we are hoping to grow half an acre in Lindsborg, Kansas, which has a rich history of broomcorn that we are helping to bring back.

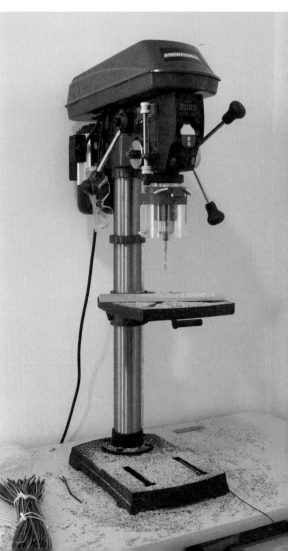

PROCESS OVERVIEW

01 Everything starts with soaking the broomcorn bales in cold water for five seconds. This makes the broomcorn pliable. I let the broomcorn sit for five minutes afterwards to allow the excess moisture to run off. It is important to ensure that nothing becomes mouldy.

02 I put the handle of the broom into the broom winder and wrap the wire around the handle. The winder is foot-powered and uses a lot of energy. The key to making a long-lasting broom is keeping the broomcorn tightly bound with lots of tension.

03 Adding the first layer of broomcorn can be the trickiest part of the process. I want to make sure it is evenly distributed around the whole handle; if it is not, the resulting broom will be unbalanced. It has taken years to get good at this. Many makers tend to use cheaper broomcorn for the inside, but I use the best quality broomcorn for the whole broom.

04 The excess broomcorn around the handle is carefully trimmed away using a specially designed eight-inch broom knife.

05 Just like humans, brooms have "shoulders", to allow for a wider sweep. I add the next layer of broomcorn to create this feature.

06 Throughout the whole process, the previous

broomcorn should be tucked out of the way before the next layer is added. I use a piece of hook-and-loop fastener to cuff the broomcorn in place. Without this it puffs out, making it harder to manipulate.

07 After the shoulders, two more layers are added to the broom that hide everything else I have done so far. These layers use a lot of broomcorn and can conceal any previous mistakes you do not want anyone to see.

08 The broom is taken out of the winder and placed in a clamp in order to flatten the head. I then make two or three rows of stitching using a double-pointed needle to maintain the shape after it is removed from the clamp. A lot of effort is needed in order to create the tension required.

09 Some brooms have a decorative braid added to the top. This is actually another piece of the broomcorn plant and is a way many broom makers add their own decorative flair to their creations. It also helps to hide unsightly marks that may occur on the handle.

10 Finally, I drill a hole and add a piece of leather to the top of the handle, allowing the broom to be hung up. Standing a broom on its bristles will shorten its lifespan. I may also add a mineral oil finish, depending on the handle.

FORGING A CAREER

Since graduating from college, it has been my goal to make broom making a full-time career. It has been a difficult path as my income is dependent on people actually buying my work. It is very hard to sustain broom making as a career, but I have just kept going at it. The hardest part is remaining motivated to keep producing. Some days you may travel to a new, unique place, but mostly you are in your workshop making as much as possible for when you do travel. I do art fairs, demonstrations, and lectures to earn a living, as well as online sales and custom orders. When you are making art the way I am, you become your brand, something for people to connect with. It is hard to just sell a broom without someone meeting me. My sales are always better when I am at an event versus having someone else trying to sell for me.

"Not only does teaching provide me with a steady source of income, but it allows me to pass on to others how to make brooms"

May until November is my busiest selling time of the year. That is when I do all my shows and have nearly eighty per cent of my sales. For the rest of the year I am hard at work making sure I have enough products to sell. My day is usually six to eight hours of actually making brooms. I often end up having someone come by who is interested in learning more about what I do. I am proud of what I have already accomplished, with brooms in at least twenty-five countries and nearly every state in the United States. I have been written about in multiple newspapers and a magazine or two. I have had the good fortune to be associated with Berea Tourism (visitberea.com), which has helped me promote myself tremendously.

At the moment I have two main projects. My woodworking friend Tim Wade and I opened a small gallery last year in The Cabin of Old Town in Berea, Kentucky. I am also helping Bethany College of Lindsborg, Kansas, establish a broom shop. I have five students at Bethany Brooms to whom I am teaching the craft. Not only does teaching provide me with a steady source of income, but it allows me to pass on to others how to make brooms.

SURVIVING IN THE MODERN WORLD

Broom making has not really changed too much in the last hundred years but has developed a lot as an art form over the past decade. Because of the internet, more people are seeing what is possible, which helps to spark people's imagination and view of what is possible and what is beautiful. You do not usually see a broom as beautiful, but if it is, then what else do you never pay attention to that can also be a wonderful piece of art? People love things that are colourful and out of the ordinary, and I get a lot of engagement on Instagram and Facebook when I post a one-of-a-kind broom.

Although I do not see a lot of sales as a direct response to my social media presence, it has led me to opportunities to do workshops and teach, which is one of my main sources of income. Many people want to experience something they have not ever done, and that has led me to offer more and more classes. This helps to keep broom making alive for future generations and expand people's knowledge about what I do. People will often buy a broom from me after taking a class because they grow to appreciate all the hard work I put into each one. Most of the time, I have standard broom series because I know they will sell relatively well. It is hard to be creative sometimes because I need to make sure I am making products that I know will sell. Sometimes I have the ability to make beautiful one-of-a-kind pieces that are going to take six months to sell. I try to create something different at least once a week to stay in the habit of trying to innovate.

Sometimes I find that my creative brooms become part of my standard brooms series. For example, I made one horseshoe broom that many people then wanted. All of the horseshoe brooms are made using a used Kentucky thoroughbred horseshoe, so people love the story and connection to a well-known part of Kentucky's culture.

CONSERVING THE CRAFT AND ITS LIVELIHOOD

It is vital that I share my art with as many people as possible. Not only so that the art of broom making exists, but so that it also thrives. No art can be static or else people will ignore it and not take it seriously. It has been my experience that people have a low opinion of broom making. I am here to say that broom making must look to the future to survive. Every time I teach someone how to make a broom I try to instil that mindset. I do not want someone making the same brooms I taught them; I want them to be creating their own brooms that will surprise and delight me with how beautiful they are.

The highest compliment to me is when someone says: "I never thought I would call a broom beautiful." That means I have been doing my job well. I am always looking to other art forms and how I can incorporate those techniques and aesthetics into my own brooms. I have even gone so far as to create what I am calling "abstract brooms" – non-functional brooms that still use broomcorn and broom-making techniques.

I believe strongly that everything can be beautiful. There is no reason a person should not fill their home with items that they appreciate. Anything can be art if someone is inspired to make it so. By making brooms the way I do, I believe I am helping inspire others to find beauty in the everyday, lowly objects you would not normally give a second glance.

BOW MAKING

The requirements of a bow vary depending on the type of archer. Instinctive archery is the most traditional form, and its masters rely on muscle memory and hand-eye coordination to shoot accurately. This type of archer tends to use traditional wooden bows such as long bows. More modern archers use a variety of bows, including recurve and more complex, compound bows, which have "sights" on them that aid with accuracy and aim. With all bows, the tiniest of physical attributes can make a huge difference to their performance, and this factor remains common between both bows of antiquity and those of modernity.

"Bow making and archery gives me a primal feeling. It is something all our ancestors did for thousands of years"

Simon van der Heijden

SIMON VAN DER HEIJDEN

Velp, The Netherlands | simonsbowcompany.com

Training: Self-taught

Simon van der Heijden initially focused on crafting wooden bows, stunning in their simplicity but highly effective when used by a skilled archer. Over time, he has also become fascinated by working with more modern materials that cater to contemporary archers as well, and has managed to successfully intertwine these with the attributes of traditional Asian horse bows, resulting in products that include benefits expected by a modern audience – low maintenance, very high arrow speed, and being easy to string (or use).

ORIGINS

My parents have a house on the edge of a very old, protected forest. It is the biggest National Park in The Netherlands. We moved to this beautiful location when I was ten years old. As a boy, I was always playing in the woods, spotting wildlife and building shelters. Of course, as a child strolling through these woods you need a bow. Soon I discovered you could make a simple bow yourself from a straight hazel branch.

From then on, I was fascinated with making my own basic bows and arrows. I started collecting information from books in the library – there was no internet at the time. I discovered that yew was the best wood for making bows, and we were fortunate to have a yew tree in our garden. I climbed it almost all the way to the top, reaching for thick, straight branches to cut. With practical help from my father, I made some incredible bows from those branches. These bows shot better than the ones I had made previously. From then on, my search for the ultimate bow began. When I became older I bought *The Traditional Bowyer's Bible* by Jim Hamm and became aware of beautiful handmade traditional wooden bows. I saved some money and bought a second-hand bandsaw. That's when it all started.

MOTIVATIONS

When I am in my own workshop making bows, I lose track of time. I am focused on the task at hand and nothing else is more important. For me this is perhaps a form of meditation. Making a bow involves different stages in the building process and it is very rewarding to be part of that whole process: selecting the raw materials, gluing them together, shaping them, sanding everything smooth and applying a finish, making the string and the leather handle, then test shooting it – and of course, also seeing customers who appreciate your time and effort in making something special for them.

These days there is a lot more awareness around making something with your own hands, from brewing your own beer to spoon carving. People appreciate handcraft more because they are interested in making something themselves as well. They know how much time and skill is required to create something beautiful.

In the traditional archery world, I try to help out other bowyers who have specific questions, and when I have questions they help me too. I try to promote related products – such as quivers and arrows – from craftspeople we know. We feel we have to compete with modern, cheaper products from Asia, which is why we try to help each other. I think it is very important we do not lose the skill of the traditional craft we know and love.

The shape and performance of traditional Asian and Middle-Eastern bows have always fascinated me. Tribes from the great plains from those areas used these bows in all their conquests and hunts. They are totally different from what you would perceive as a conventional wooden bow like a long bow – for me they are the racing cars of traditional bows. They are shorter for comfort on horseback or in the woods, and static tips (where the ends of the bow are made less flexible in order to influence the power of the draw) make them smooth, silent, and incredibly powerful. They are traditionally made from wood, sinew, and horn glued together. These materials handle tension and compression (the two forces in a working bow) much better than wood alone. For me as a bow maker, making such a bow was a big challenge: a shorter bow has to bend as much as a longer bow but over a shorter amount of space, meaning that there is more tension and compression on the materials and construction over a smaller area. This stores more energy when created with skill, which then transfers to the arrow. Through trial and error, I made my modern version of a "horse bow", which has the same performance as a true horse bow but also has the benefits of a modern bow suitable for modern strings and shooting light, carbon arrows.

I get a lot of long-term satisfaction when making bows. I have made a lot, but when I hold a finished bow in my hands I still think: "I made this!"

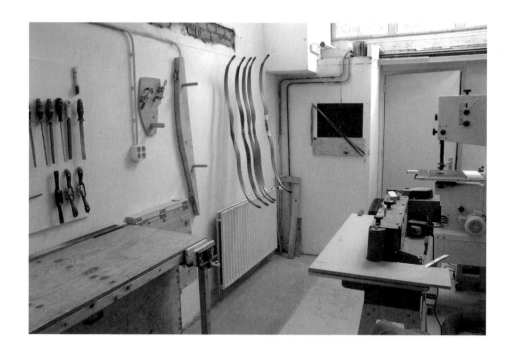

WORKSPACE AND TOOLS

I transformed my garage at home into a small workshop with a beautiful skylight. The roof is insulated and there is a small radiator which keeps the workshop warm during the winter. My stationary machines are on wheels so that I can move them around easily, and all the hand tools I need hang on the wall in front of my workbench. I try to keep my workshop clean and organized, which makes working there more efficient and pleasant.

I cannot do without the dust collector, or my bandsaw and edge-belt sander. There is a large wooden box, which is my "hotbox" or "bow oven". The bow is glued, pressed in the form, and then it goes in the hotbox to cure the glue at 80°C (176°F). This strengthens the glue bond and prevents delamination (a bow is made out of different layers, or laminations, such as bamboo, fibreglass, and wood glued together; delamination refers to when these layers come apart on the glue line). The bandsaw is used to cut out the handle and the static tips from wood, and to cut out the glued bow. I use an Uddeholm saw blade for wood and a carbide saw blade for laminated bows made from fibreglass, wood, and bamboo. With the belt sander, I sand the handle and tips to fit the glue form and to roughly shape the cut-out glued bow. From then on, I only use hand tools. I have different files for shaping the handle of the bow and a special convex palm plane to shape the siyahs (tips) of the bow.

PROCESS OVERVIEW

01 I select wood for the handle and the siyahs. I use mainly black locust, cherry, and ash. The wood has to be free from flaws, such as cracks or knots. The limbs of the bow (that is, the working section of the bow, where it bends and the energy it stored) are made from fibreglass and action bamboo (thin strips of bamboo glued vertically together to make a very tough laminate).

02 The handle and siyahs are cut with the bandsaw and sanded on the edge sander so that they exactly match the surface of the glue form. The glue form dictates the shape of the bow and consists of a bottom piece that matches the shape of the bow exactly, and a top piece that holds everything in place.

03 Once the fibreglass and action bamboo laminates have been cut to the correct length, they are dried in the hotbox.

04 I lay out each laminate, wipe down all the glue surfaces with acetone, then mix two-part epoxy glue and spread this over all mating surfaces. The wood is now ready for the glue form.

05 The laminates, handle, and siyahs are placed in the glue form, and covered by a rubber strip. The top piece of the glue form secures the laminates, rubber strip, and a deflated air hose in place. Gradually the air hose is filled with air to around 65 PSI to apply the required pressure to glue the laminates together. The whole form is placed in the hotbox to cure the glue at 80°C (176°F) within four hours. After the glue has dried, the laminates hold the shape they are glued in.

06 When the form is cooled to room temperature, I take the bow out of the form. With a template, I draw the shape on the back of the bow, making sure it is straight, then cut it out

on the bandsaw. I use an edge sander to roughly shape it.

07 I glue Micarta (a composite of linen in thermosetting plastic) to the tips for the string nocks (where the string will be attached), which makes the bow fast and safe for modern non-stretch string material. I shape the siyahs and cut out the string nocks.

08 When stringing the bow for the first time, I ensure there is no limb twist and that the tiller is correct (balanced). The bow limb has to bend towards the archer when the bow is drawn. If the bow limb turns sideways (left or right), it twists and can break. Measuring the tiller is a way of ensuring that the bend of the bow as the string is drawn is correct. I sand the limbs until the bow has the desired draw weight (this is the amount of force required to pull the string back to the necessary position to shoot the arrow).

09 I then sand the whole bow smooth and sign it with a serial number, draw weight, and draw length (this indicates the distance between the nocking point and the pivot point on the string once the string is drawn). Multiple coats of two-part spray finish can now be applied.

10 When the finish is dry, I sew on the leather handle and make the string. The string is made from two materials: very thin strands of HMPE (high-modulus polyethylene) and serving cord, which is made from nylon. The draw weight of the bow determines the number of strands used for the string. The nylon protects the string from wear at the string grooves and where the arrow is nocked on. Finally, the bow is finished.

FORGING A CAREER

I teach high-school children with special needs three days a week. The other three days I am in my workshop, and for one day I try to do nothing. I am constantly busy – when I do not have too many orders, I build up my stock. Although I make custom bows, some customers cannot wait for them, or afford them, so buy from stock. I never attend shows or markets and only sell online or through dealers. You have to experience my bows to appreciate the craftsmanship and understand the difference when compared to less expensive versions. All my dealers have my bows in store for customers to test. The Netherlands is a small country with an even smaller traditional archery community. I sell almost only to other European countries like Germany, Austria, and the United Kingdom, and also to Southeast Asia, mainly Indonesia.

My average working day starts with my girlfriend and me walking our dog. We then eat breakfast and I check my emails. I go to my workshop and put on my apron – mostly I know what I have to do, but sometimes I have a to-do list. I do the intricate jobs in the morning such as cutting out bows, shaping tips, and stringing and balancing bows. Around noon I walk the dog again, eat lunch, and check my emails and social media. My afternoon involves less demanding tasks like sanding a bow, making handles, or preparing for the next day. I finish at around five o'clock, although in the evening I sometimes make one or two strings or try to do some social media.

Because I do not want to give up teaching right now, I only have two or three days a week to make bows. If I had more time I could of course build more bows, learn new woodworking techniques to allow me to work faster, and spend more time on social media. Although it is beautiful, my workspace is a little limited and I am not currently in the financial position to rent a large space somewhere close to home. My workshop is at home and I like that a lot. I do not have to travel, I just go through two doors and I can start working. I want to make my livelihood work for me, and at the moment it does.

It is important to be surrounded by creative, open-minded people who can help me and who I can help. Freelancers and those who have their own company understand the struggles, the stress, but also the excitement and drive needed to start something yourself. Making a living has almost nothing to do with your craft. I make beautiful bows, but there are a lot of beautiful bows out there. A lot of people are used to buying things of less quality that will not last as long as those made by skilled craftspeople. This is reflected in the price. I hope in the future people will buy less, but what they buy will be long lasting, beautiful, and have value because of the story it holds. One of the most important things is that I love doing what I do, being by myself in my workshop, making something beautiful. If you are driven by money, you will not succeed. As with most crafts, I am not going to become rich from making bows. It is my passion, and a Rolex around my wrist would only be uncomfortable when sanding or sawing.

SURVIVING IN THE MODERN WORLD

The traditional bows I make are used mainly for instinctive archery. The shape, appearance, and shooting experience are the same as those of the bows our ancestors used. The difference between my bows and those from the past however is in the materials, which cater to a modern audience, and construction time. I developed a few modern woodworking techniques, such as working with a pattern router and template so as to always match the handle to the form, and to make some tasks less time consuming. I use fibreglass, carbon, and modern glues to make my bows maintenance free, easy to string, and safer to use. They are suited for fast-flight strings, which are made from a non-stretch material and are therefore very demanding on the bow. As mentioned, my bows can also be shot with very light, modern carbon arrows. These are the demands of my customer, the modern archer.

Another way I have adapted to a modern audience is by making the most of social media, which is key for a small business. It is a relatively easy and cheap way of showing what you do to a large group of people. For example, Instagram helped me to reach a lot of customers in Indonesia, which I never thought was possible. The downside is you have to keep posting and engaging. The demand for high-quality photos and short videos is high on social media; the bar is raised constantly so you have to keep up to show off your skills. This is something a craftsperson, and any small business, has to keep in mind.

CONSERVING THE CRAFT AND ITS LIVELIHOOD

My grandfather did a lot of woodworking as a pastime when he retired, mostly furniture making and wood carving. When I was small I was often with him in his workshop, helping him or making something with him. I was a bit too young to really learn true woodworking skills but I think it had an impact on me. Bow making for me was a long process of trial and error. I had to "invent the wheel" for myself with many techniques and possibilities, but trial and error is one of the best learning experiences. However, a lifetime is almost too short to excel in something. It is important to pass on your knowledge and skills, as then the next generation of craftspeople do not have to go through the whole process again and are able to start at a higher level. Bow making and archery give me a primal feeling. It is something all our ancestors did for thousands of years. It makes a connection with who we really are. It gives me peace and lets me be in the moment.

Making something with your hands or similar, such as programming, filming, and writing, is very important for us humans. Creating something involves learning new skills and techniques – when you finally master something, it is very satisfying. If you have never experienced this feeling, the chance is that your life feels unfulfilled. With this in mind, I think it is important for people to learn crafts and discover the love of being creative with their minds and their hands.

HANDSEWN SHOEMAKING

The craft of handsewn shoemaking dates back as far as the sixteenth century, with very little of the method changing in that time. Beneficiaries of the shoes experience a bespoke fit from a workflow that incorporates over two hundred steps using only handheld tools – a process that requires infinite patience and passion.

"Bespoke shoemaking is known as the 'gentle craft', yet it is physically demanding, methodical, and very exacting"

Deborah Carré

CARRÉDUCKER

London, UK | carreducker.com

Training: Full-time apprenticeships with a master shoemaker

Since 2004, from their workshops at Cockpit Arts in London, Deborah Carré and James Ducker (together forming the brand Carréducker) have been making beautiful, bespoke handsewn shoes for men, using centuries-old traditional techniques they have each learned and nurtured over the last two decades. As self-appointed "guardians of the trade", they continue to champion the making of shoes without a machine.

ORIGINS

James and I both came to shoemaking as a second career. I had fallen in love with the craft while developing my degree collection with R. E. Tricker in Northampton, but in 1997, I was fortunate enough to win a scholarship with the coveted Queen Elizabeth Scholarship Trust to train with master shoemaker Paul Wilson, and soon swapped my office desk for a shoemaking bench.

James joined Paul's workshop soon after. Prior to this, he had been teaching Business English in Spain, and was attracted to the idea of shoemaking when one of his students revealed their father was a master cordwainer. James began his shoemaking journey at the Shoe Makers Guild School, Barcelona, before returning to London where he was accepted as an apprentice at John Lobb (a respected shoemaking company established in 1866).

Our paths continued in parallel for some time. I set up my own small business – Atelier Carré – and was a visiting lecturer in Accessories Design & Marketing at University of the Arts, London, while James had become a fully fledged maker for Lobb, and was teaching handsewn shoemaking at Cordwainers College, London. We finally joined forces to found Carréducker in December 2004.

MOTIVATIONS

Bespoke shoemaking is known as the "gentle craft", yet it is physically demanding, methodical, and very exacting, so it does attract a certain character. I am naturally quite volatile and impatient, but shoemaking doesn't tolerate either. If you get too hot and bothered your threads stick – or worse, break, and your knife cuts where it shouldn't. I have therefore had to learn infinite patience and to enjoy the two hundred steps involved in making each pair of shoes. For James, however, shoemaking encourages an almost meditative state; when the stitching is flowing well he finds it relaxing, allowing him time to think and daydream. We are great examples of why, historically, shoemakers have a reputation for being either philosophers or revolutionaries... or both!

James and I may have very different personalities, but we are drawn to and enjoy the craft for similar reasons: the high quality of the natural oak bark and vegetable-tanned leather that we work with; the satisfaction of seeing a pair of shoes evolve from an initial sketch to a finished pair; and the wonderful network of highly skilled craftspeople that we work with.

"Much as we enjoy making beautiful shoes, our favourite and most memorable ones are those that have a positive impact on the customer"

We particularly enjoy teaching; helping beginners to make their first pair of shoes using handheld tools or adding to the skill sets of experienced shoemakers. Handsewn shoemaking has changed very little over the centuries. Although the techniques may vary from maker to maker and country to country, it has a proven track record dating back to the sixteenth century, so we extol the virtues of making shoes without a machine.

People often ask what our most memorable or favourite pair of shoes is. Much as we enjoy making beautiful shoes, our favourite and most memorable ones are those that have a positive impact on the customer – whether it be them walking in comfort for the first time, or the new-found confidence that their shoes inspire.

Thanks to organizations like the Independent Shoemakers, the Heritage Craft Association, the Queen Elizabeth Scholarship Trust, and Walpole, we have had the good fortune to meet and get to know many other talented craftspeople from around the world – and through social media we are now able to keep up with and support one another online.

WORKSPACE AND TOOLS

We have made shoes everywhere from a tiny brick shed to a chilly industrial unit off the motorway, but Cockpit Arts has been home to Carréducker from the outset.

BBC Radio 6 Music plays in the background and the air is rich with the aroma of oak-bark leather from Bakers in Devon (one of Britain's last remaining traditional oak-bark tanneries); a set of velvet-seated, cut-down chairs and a low workbench are at the centre; the walls are hung with customers' wooden shoe lasts (a last is a wooden mould around which a shoe is built), and steel shelves hold shoes in varying stages of construction. Framed press coverage, our Marsh Heritage Crafts "Made in Britain" Award, Balvenie Masters of Craft Award, and QEST Award for Excellence are an important reminder of our successes so far; and pride of place is a peg board holding the armoury of specialist tools peculiar to our craft.

The most important of these tools is the shoemaker's knife – used for almost everything – from carving through great bends of quarter-inch thick, oak-bark leather, to finely shaping the heel on a dress shoe. There are also sharp awls for making stitch holes; lasting pincers to stretch the leather over the lasts; a French hammer to gently mould the leather to the last; a sleeking bone for smoothing out wrinkles; and a tool roll of edge and heel irons – their wooden handles worn to the shape of the craftsman's hand.

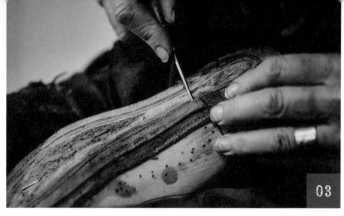

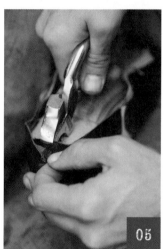

PROCESS OVERVIEW

01 After we have met the customer, our last maker carves a pair of wooden lasts to the customer's measurements and specification. Once these are ready, we cover the left last with masking tape and draw on the chosen design. This provides a master for the pattern cutter to work from.

02 The pattern cutter then transforms the drawing into paper pattern pieces for the closer. In turn, the closer clicks (cuts out) the pattern pieces from the leather and closes them (stitches them together).

03 We are now ready to see the customer for a series of fittings. Once the fit is right, we handsew the shoes at our workbench. First, oak-bark leather insoles are nailed to the underside of the

lasts and allowed to dry; then they are trimmed, and a ridge called a holdfast is cut from each one. An awl is used to make holes through the ridge for stitching.

04 Next, all internal components are cut from oak-bark tanned belly leather. These are soaked, mellowed, and skived (shaved thinner) with a knife.

05 The uppers are then fitted with stiffeners at the heel and toe puffs at the toes, between the lining and upper. These components give shape to the shoe, hold it on the foot, and protect the toes. The uppers are then lasted over (pulled onto the lasts with pliers and fixed with nails).

06 A welt is prepared, which is a strip of leather that goes around the outside of the shoe and

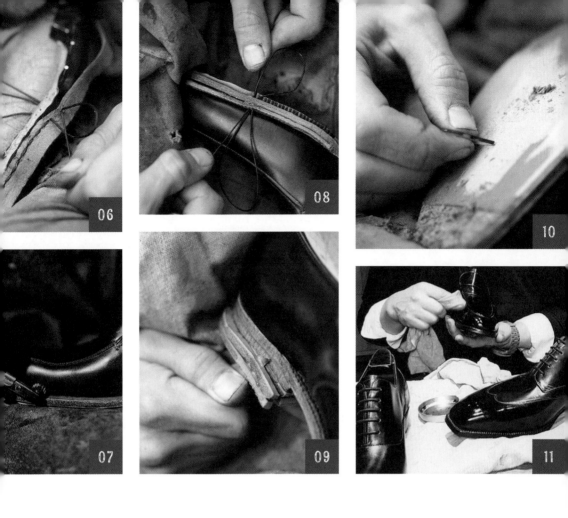

attaches the sole to the upper. Two five-cord threads are made from twisted hemp, which are then waxed and attached with bristles (flexible needles). The welt is stitched to the side of the shoe through the upper, lining, and holdfast.

07 Cork (to fill in any spaces) and a leather shank (for internal strength) are fitted. An oak-bark leather sole is cut out, soaked, hammered, and glued in place. A fudge wheel is used to mark the number of stitches per inch on the welt.

08 A channel (flap of leather) is cut into the sole leather and the sole is hand-stitched to the welt. The sole edges are shaped, and the channel is glued down to hide the stitches.

09 The heel is then built layer by layer with paste and nails, starting with a horse-shoe-shaped piece of leather called a split lift. The final piece of leather is called the top piece and is usually made of rubber and leather for durability.

10 Then the edges are blended and smoothed with a rasp, glass, and three grades of sandpaper. The sole edges are set (shaped and hardened) with a hot edge iron. The sole is glassed and smoothed with sandpaper. The soles and heels are then finished – either burnished with polish or inked and waxed.

11 Finally the lasts are removed and the shoes are cleaned, nourished, and polished.

FORGING A CAREER

When we founded Carréducker, we knew that we would have to do things differently to gain traction in a market dominated by a small number of well-established, centuries-old companies. Rather than go in with a bespoke offering at the start, we initially designed and launched a made-to-order service of handsewn shoes and boots in standard UK sizes, for customers to try on and order. They were made with the same craftsmanship as a bespoke offering, but at a keen price point and a faster turnaround.

We then thought bespoke customers might be interested in commissioning across a variety of luxury items, so organized a series of Bespoke Club evenings to showcase our work and invited like-minded businesses to co-host with us. We also promoted our work to the press and attracted great support, helping to raise our profile and build brand credibility. We received support from the UK's luxury industry body, Walpole, as part of its business mentoring programme. We were also invited to deliver a bespoke shoe service at Gieves & Hawkes (gievesandhawkes.com) with our workshop on the shop floor.

Being able to demonstrate the craft is still a key part of our marketing. Over the years we have demonstrated our skills at numerous craft events – alongside other Queen Elizabeth Scholarship Trust scholars at St James' and Hampton Court Palaces; at Origin, the London contemporary craft fair; in the Crafts Council's *Added Value* exhibition; at Vicheron Constantin *Makers of Excellence*; and in the shop window at No.1 Savile Row during London Craft Week – and we are now part of the permanent exhibition at the Design Museum London, where our film shows a pair of boots being handsewn from start to finish.

Gradually, the demand for full bespoke grew from our initial foray and has continued to grow organically ever since. However, it became clear early on that we couldn't rely on bespoke to sustain the business or to enable us to grow as we wanted, and that we needed to add more strings to our bow.

Carréducker now encompasses four strands, each with the handsewn craft at its core. As well as the bespoke service at Gieves & Hawkes and James Purdey and Sons, we have established ourselves as the leading provider of handsewn shoemaking courses and classes in the UK through our shoemaking school; we sell shoemaking tools and materials online; and we have run a series of successful crowdfunding campaigns to launch limited edition, ready-to-wear shoes and boots, manufactured here in England by artisanal producers, and sold online direct to the consumer.

Social media allows mavericks like us to have a global shop front and gives our various audiences a taster of our amazing craft, whether it be bespoke customers or potential students. We are always thrilled when we get an email from a novice maker who has made a pair of shoes with the blog as their guide.

Through our school, we are often asked for advice about starting shoemaking or getting into the industry. Our advice is usually this: try one of our courses to see if handsewn shoemaking really is for you – it is harder work than you think; if you love it, then keep making for fun, friends, and family. If you love it and have an aptitude, then keep making and get yourself an apprenticeship or scholarship to learn more. But always remember: it will reward you in many ways, but not always financially!

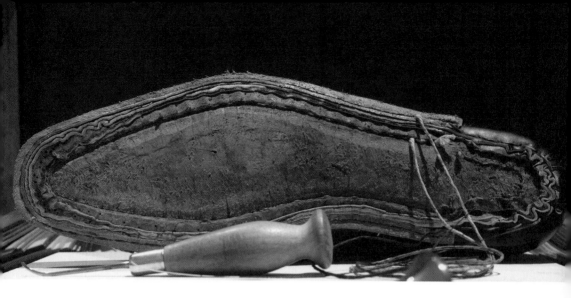

SURVIVING IN THE MODERN WORLD

We realize how fortunate we are to have pursued our passion for shoemaking and to have built and maintained a business from it, but it has not been without its challenges. We found it hard to meet new customers at the start and orders only came about by attending events and networking, meeting people face to face or being recommended by word of mouth – a painful process as we are both quite shy! Thankfully, social media has been a complete game changer. It gives even the most remote craftsperson a shop window to a global audience; today's craftsperson must be as skilled on Instagram as they are at the workbench.

We have also had to respond to a changing customer base. Although the traditional bespoke shoe customer remains, there is a whole new world of customers for whom bespoke does not mean a straight toe-cap, black Oxford (a type of shoe) – men confident of their personal style and not shy of colour. So, although we pride ourselves on making a beautiful pair of welted shoes using centuries-old traditional techniques, we have now added rubber and crepe sole choices to the bespoke service and offer customers the chance to have all their footwear manufactured on their bespoke lasts – all without compromising on the quality of the final product of course.

The choice of styles available on our courses has also broadened as we have introduced shorter classes in hand-lasting and hand-welting, again without compromising on the craftsmanship involved.

There is quite a lot going on, which begs the question, when do we have time to design or to make shoes? The answer has been to reorganize the structure of Carréducker, opening a dedicated school in Shoreditch and growing the team with external shoemakers and lecturers. It is a big step for us, but we feel it is the right one to keep growing at a pace that feels appropriate.

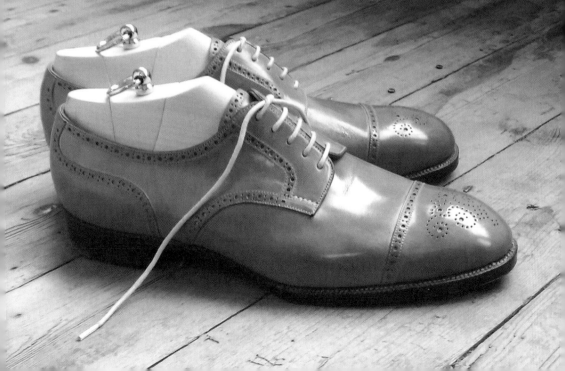

CONSERVING THE CRAFT AND ITS LIVELIHOOD

Passing on knowledge is at the heart of Carréducker. We believe it is vital to keep the skills and techniques of the craft alive, not for the sake of it, but because it is a craft that still has much to offer. We extol the benefits of handsewn shoes to customers – best-quality materials; durable and repairable construction; low environmental impact, and so on. We enthuse about learning the craft to students – that they can make a wearable pair of shoes from day one, with minimal tools and using the best materials.

From a personal level, we know only too well the benefits of shared knowledge and experience. We would not be here without the generosity of the craftsman who taught us; the makers who let us sit beside them at their benches watching them work; the support and advice of our specialist suppliers; and our colleagues in the industry who we can ask a question of at any point in time. Over the years, we have mentored and encouraged hundreds of enthusiasts, academics, and practitioners ourselves; sharing the heritage techniques of handsewn shoemaking – meeting wonderful people, learning new techniques ourselves, and enjoying fascinating conversations along the way.

We officially took up the mantle of teaching the craft in London when Cordwainers College closed its course in 2006, and today the Carréducker Shoe Making School attracts students from around the world. Many are beginners enjoying a creative holiday or keen to learn to make shoes for family and friends, and others already have some experience and want to become handsewn shoemakers themselves or to enhance existing skills. Whatever their reasons, we try to encourage and support their passion without sugar-coating the reality that being a craftsperson in the twenty-first century is very hard work. That said, it is enormously satisfying.

GLOSSARY

Adze

A woodworking tool similar to an axe except that the blade is perpendicular to the handle. Used for shaping, hollowing, and flattening wood.

Angle grinder

A handheld grinding tool with interchangeable grinding discs. Used to grind at any angle.

Awl

A pointed tool used to prick holes through leather.

Bandsaw

A saw in which the cutting blade is a continuous band that runs between two or more wheels, providing a continuous, uniform, unidirectional cutting motion.

Bent knife

A knife used for hollowing out wood, especially when making spoons and bowls. Sometimes called a spoon or crook knife.

Bevel

Where the edge of an object has a sloped rather than a square edge. Sometimes also called chamfer, it is a technique often used in craft to enhance and soften the appearance of an object's edges.

Bevel and square

These are two measuring tools that can be used as guides when drilling or shaping a material. A square is always ninety degrees and a bevel or sliding bevel can be moved to whatever is the desired angle.

Billet

A simple piece of angular wood that has been split out from a larger piece. A billet is often the first stage in many green woodworking projects, such as spoon carving. You can also have metal billets in blacksmithing.

Billhook

A traditional hand tool with a hook-shaped blade, used generally for cutting and clearing smaller live wood stems and branches.

Bodger

The term for a traditional green woodworker.

Bowie knife

A hunting knife, named after legendary frontiersman James Bowie, who carried, hunted, and fought with one in the nineteenth century.

Bowl gouge

The metal tool used to gouge out the shape of the bowl during the turning (see page 316) process.

Bushcraft

Also called wilderness skills. This is the knowledge of and techniques for surviving in the outdoors that have evolved and been passed on for centuries.

Butt joint

The most basic of woodworking joints where two pieces of wood are joined together as shown in the illustration below.

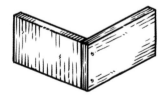

Coppicing

A traditional method of managing woodlands by cutting back trees to ground level to stimulate new growth. Repeated on cycles every few years to maximize the woodland harvest of usable timber.

Drawknife

A symmetrical two-handed knife, with a handle at each end. The blade is drawn towards the user to remove shavings and shape the wood. Often used in conjunction with a shaving horse.

Drill press

A fixed drilling machine/tool that gives more accuracy than a hand drill. Often attached to a bench or floor standing.

F-clamps

A clamp whose side profile is an "F" shape and is adjustable, meaning it is often used on larger scale objects. C- and G-clamps are also very common.

Fid

A tool that is used to separate strands of rope and untie knots.

Froe

A traditional tool used for splitting wood. More controlled than an axe, it is a preferred tool for crafting items such as roof shingles/shakes (wooden roof tiles). It allows one to control the direction of the split by levering to one side or the other, rather than simply driving a wedge through the wood. Also known as a shingle knife.

Grain

The fibres in wood create the "grain" and run along the length of tree trunks and branches. When it comes to working wood, you can either "go with" or "go against" the grain. Going with the grain truncates the fibres and makes it easier to produce a cleaner result, whereas going against the grain will often catch and tear the wood.

Green wood

Fresh or recently cut wood which is worked on before the sap dries out, making it softer and therefore easier to work with using hand tools.

Hew

To chop a material (especially wood) with a tool such as an axe, typically to work it into a desired shape, such as a square beam from a log.

Kaolin

A type of clay.

Lathe

A machine used for shaping material by rotating it, simultaneously allowing the user to hold cutting tools against the rotating material to shape it.

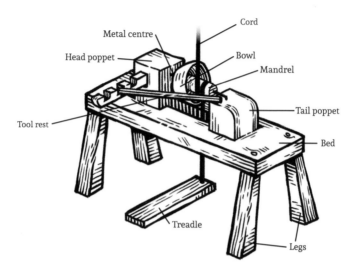

Leg vice

A holding device usually located on the face of a workbench and used to secure jobs in a way that makes it easy to work on the edges.

Mortise

Usually one half of a "mortise and tenon" joint, the mortise is the recess or hole in which the corresponding tenon fits.

Nail chuck

On a lathe, a nail chuck works as a mandrel to hold the piece being worked on while rotation occurs.

Pair of dividers

An instrument used for measuring and transferring distances.

Patina
In regard to leather, a patina is the effect created as leather ages and is subject to environmental factors such as oils from your skin and natural wear and tear. Most noticeable is the change in colour, for example from a clean tan to a darker brown.

Pith
The soft, spongy part (parenchyma cells) usually located in the middle of the stem/trunk of wood.

Press knife
A tool that can be used to cut leather and other materials.

Sacking needle
A strong needle used for stitching heavy-duty material such as sacking and leather.

Scorp
Similar to a drawknife but the blade is curved to allow the user to create rounded shapes, such as hollows where one sits on a chair seat.

Scribe
A tool used to mark out a shape or design. A carbide scribe is hard enough to be able to mark steel.

Shaving horse
A traditional woodworking bench. The woodworker (bodger) sits astride it, and uses a leg-operated clamp to hold the wood, freeing up both hands to shape the wood with hand tools such as a drawknife.

Sloyd
Crafting techniques generally used for green woodworking which were formed and refined in Scandinavian areas from 1865 onwards. Derived from the Swedish word *Slöjd*, which translates as handcraft.

Spoke shave
A tool used for smoothing and refining wood.

Steam-bending
A process of heating wood using steam. The steam allows the wood to become pliable enough to bend into a new shape, which then sets as the wood cools.

Tail vice
A tail vice is designed to hold a job securely to the top of a bench in order to work on the wider face surfaces of the job.

Tang
On a knife, the part of the blade that goes into the handle.

Tempering
A process of heating and cooling metal to increase the material's strength and durability.

Tenon

Usually one half of a "mortise and tenon" joint, the tenon is the projection that fits into the corresponding mortise (hole) on the other side of the joint.

Travisher

A tool consisting of a curved piece of wood and a blade that is used to finely shape wood.

Treadle

A way of powering a machine by working a foot-operated lever.

Truss

A framework often used in roof construction. A common truss has a triangular shape.

Turning

To shape wood by using a mechanism to turn (spin) the wood. The cutting tool is then held against the moving wood to remove shavings. Bowl turning is one of the most common forms.

Windsor chair

A chair constructed from a solid timber seat into which the legs and back supports are inserted separately from each other as tenons into drilled mortises. The illustration below shows a rocking Windsor chair, although not all Windsor chairs are rockers.

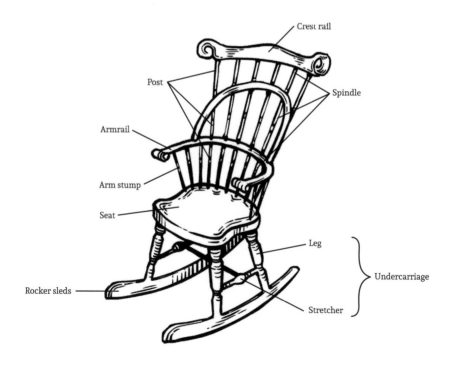

ACKNOWLEDGEMENTS

Opening pages	p. 3 © 3dtotal.com Ltd; p. 4 © Michael McLaughlin; p. 6 © Herzflimmern – Nadine Schachinger; p. 8 © 3dtotal.com Ltd; p. 20 © EJ Osborne
Foreword	All photos © Giles W Bennett
My Journey into the Woods	All photos © 3dtotal.com Ltd
Blacksmithing	pp. 22, 27 (top right), 28, 29 (top left), 32 (image 10), 36 © Nathaniel Forest
	pp. 24, 26, 27 (top left; bottom), 29 (all except top left), 30, 31, 32 (images 08 and 09), 33, 34 (top left; bottom), 37, 38 (bottom) © Louie Sal-long
	p. 34 (top right) © Karen Rudolph
	p. 38 (top) © Emily Christie
Knife making	All photos © 3dtotal.com Ltd
Axe making	pp. 63 (middle left), 64–65 (images 01, 02, 03, and 05), 68, 70, 71 © Kaspars Kurcens
	pp.58, 62, 63 (top right, bottom left), 64 (image 04), 69 (bottom) © Jānis Škapars/TVNET
	All other photos © Autine Tools
Woodworking	All photos © EJ Osborne
Spoon carving	pp. 90, 93 (middle), 95 (top right), 98, 103 © Michael McLaughlin
	All other photos © Éamonn O'Sullivan
Woodturning	pp. 104, 109, 111, 112 (images 01, 02, 03, and 04), 117, 118 (top, bottom left) ® Yoav Elkayam
	pp. 106, 110 ® Adi Segal www.adi-segal.com
	pp. 112 (image 05), 113 (images 06, 07, 08, and 09), 114, 116, 119 ® Catarina Seixas
	p. 120, 123 (top), 124, 125, 126, 127, 128 (top), 131 (top), 133 © Herzflimmern – Nadine Schachinger
	All other photos © Franz Josef Keilhofer

"Craft's relevance within the context of human civilization will allow it to continue as a field of exploration as long as artists are willing to carry its history"

Mitch Iburg